AND I LIVED TO TELL THE TALES

THE LIFE OF A FIGHTER PILOT

BY

LT. COL. ED COBLEIGH
CALL SIGN "FAST EDDIE"

MW00700298

And I Lived to Tell the Tales: The Life of a Fighter Pilot (First Edition)
© Copyright 2022 Ed Cobleigh

This book published by Check Six Books of Paso Robles, CA.

For rights, media & contact visit: **www.EdCobleigh.com**

ISBN: 978-1629672380
Library of Congress Control Number: 2022907311

All rights reserved. No part of this book may be reproduced in any form or by any electronic or mechanical means, including information storage and retrieval systems, without written permission from the author, except in the case of a reviewer, who may quote brief passages embodied in critical articles or in a review.

Trademarked names may appear throughout this book. Rather than use a trademark symbol with every occurrence of a trademarked name, names are used in an editorial fashion, with no intention of infringement of the respective owner's trademark.

Produced for Check Six Books by Brian Schwartz (USA)
Book cover by Bespoke Book Covers LTD, UK

All inquiries directed to Check Six Books, 3750 Sky Ridge Drive, Paso Robles, CA, 93446, USA

Other books by Ed Cobleigh:

War for the Hell of It: A Fighter Pilot's View of Vietnam

The Pilot: Fighter Planes and Paris Times

The First Fighter Pilot-Roland Garros: The Life and of the Playboy Who Invented Air Combat

Fly with the Falcon: Love, Loss, Liberty

Rev 5.5

DEDICATION

To Those Who Lost Their Lives Along the Way

Prologue
PRE-MISSION BRIEFING

Listen Up, Pogues!

This book is both a prequel and a sequel to my best-selling memoir, *War for the Hell of It: A Fighter Pilot's View of Vietnam.* That earlier book is an account of adventures I experienced while losing the Vietnam War. One aspect of writing for a partial target audience of fighter pilots is you get immediate, direct, often frank feedback, sometimes accompanied by an imaginary index finger-poke in the chest. Fighter pilots, myself included, are not shy about telling you what they think.

One recurring theme in the reviews and emails I received concerning *War for the Hell of It* was an oft-stated desire for more flying stories and fewer political statements. Writing about the Vietnam War without getting into the dysfunctional enabling politics would be like writing about a fish, a flounder seems the most apt analogy, without mentioning water. However, I hoisted aboard the many freely-offered comments. This book is the result; more aviation tales, less politics, and the inside story of what it was like for me as a fighter pilot.

What follows is a series of vignettes about my career as a fighter pilot with the United States Air Force, the United States Navy, the Royal Air Force, the Imperial Iranian Air Force, and the French Air Force. Some people just have trouble holding a steady job. Did each tale happen precisely as described? Probably not exactly. This account was written from my memory of events most of which occurred over 50 years ago. Non-flying tales are also included to break up the airborne string.

Our memories tend to be highly selective. As we look back at our past, we usually recall only the triumphs and successes, forgetting the failures and the foul-ups. You can't remember in your school days when you struck out with the bases loaded or when your girlfriend dumped you. In your mental server reside warm sepia shaded images of when you scored on the baseball diamond or at the drive-in movie theatre (do you remember those dimly-lit dens of seduction?). I tried to take into account this mental phenomenon and not just re-tell those flying yarns which cast my contributions to the chronicled events in a complementary light. I also included the times when things did not go at all well. Fortunately, in my flying career there were any number of screw-ups available for review to balance out the win-loss scoreboard.

Another sadder recurring episode in this book is the loss of life of a fellow aviator. Fighter aviation is inherently hazardous, the skies are fraught with peril. Throughout my career, the loss of fellow pilots through crashes echoed as a constant drumbeat. You can't avoid covering those losses and be true to history. I couldn't have dishonored the dead by omitting their stories, however tragic. Few professions include losing a small but constant percentage of friends to violent deaths every year.

In the timeframe of this book, the three most dangerous occupations in the United States of America were commercial fisherman, coal miner, and fighter pilot. A naval aviator operating off aircraft carriers, if he flew for a full 20-year career, which few did, ran a 23% chance of busting his ass. Not a great recruiting pitch. I like to tell folks of the three listed most hazardous occupations, I worked in two. Mind you, I think commercial fishing fatalities were more common in the Gulf of Alaska's mountainous, icy seas than when running trot lines for catfish on the Tennessee River with my uncle.

As you turn these pages, keep in mind the adage: "What is the difference between a war story and a fairy tale?" Answer: "A fairy tale begins with "Once upon a time….." A war story, which the US Navy calls a sea story, starts with "There I was….." That's the principal difference.

Also notable in these stories is the happenings are of a unisex nature. At the time, just after the middle of the last century, women's roles in the military flying services were non-existent. It was a man's game, hence the preponderance of the words "guys" and "men" in the chapters to follow. Women were confined to the domains of Intelligence, Weather, Administration, and Nursing. Today, all flying slots and all combat missions are open to female aviators. Women are fighter pilots, flight instructors, squadron and wing commanders, generals, and demo pilots. The USAF aerial demo team, the Thunderbirds, has a female pilot flying in airshows. This is called progress. It is a good thing. We need more women aviators.

Besides "There I was," all good verbal flying stories begin with a well-known phrase, "This Is No Shit," abbreviated as TINS. Many a tale of aerial daring-do related at the bar and illustrated by an aviator waving his, or her, hands, over-G'ing a wrist watch, begins with, "This is no shit." I tried to write this tome in a familiar vernacular, as if I were standing at the bar, glass of Tennessee Whiskey firmly in hand, talking to the reader one-on-one.

So, climb aboard, strap in, and let's go fly fighter planes.

TINS!

CHAPTER ONE
UNDERGRADUATE PILOT TRAINING, WEBB AFB, BIG SPRING, TX, 1966

Dreams Come True in a Bug Smasher

I can't remember ever not wanting to be a pilot, some kind of pilot. Since I was a wee lad, I have built model airplanes. I watched the action at the local airport. I read every aviation-themed book I could get my hands on particularly liking memoirs and first-hand accounts. Ernest K. Gann, Richard S. Bach, Arthur Gould Lee, and James Salter filled my young head with tales of aerial derring-do. I read and re-read *Fighting the Flying Circus,* an account of WWI air combat elegantly ghost-written for Eddie Rickenbacker. (Captain Eddie dropped out of school after the eighth grade. He wasn't known for his erudition). My burning ambition was to fly, preferably with the United States Air Force, the USAF, as a dashing fighter pilot. Is there any other kind? But, I was prepared to settle for being the steely-eyed captain of an airliner on international runs. Having devoured book after book about the Battle of Britain, I revered those Royal Air Force fighter pilots. I felt there was no way I could join them. I was wrong.

My father, also named Ed Cobleigh, a retired US Army Colonel, was worried my dreams might come true. He saw pilots come back from WWII with no skills other than flying a plane. With the over-supply of aviators in the post-war job market, many ended up hanging around bars looking for flying work.

In my youngish mind's eye, I saw myself flying a SPAD XIII, white silk scarf blowing in the slipstream (WWI and WWII fighter pilots wore silk scarfs to protect their necks from chaffing against the stiff collars of leather flying jackets. Also, it looked way cool). I engaged in swirling dogfights with the Red Baron over the Western Front. I pictured myself running to my Spitfire during a Battle of Britain scramble, getting airborne to have a go at the Jerries. Ice water in my veins, I patrolled MiG Alley in a F-86 Sabrejet like James Salter. Most often, I saw myself as an intrepid F-104 Starfighter pilot for the Tennessee Air National Guard, defending the Volunteer State from all aerial invaders.

During high school, I couldn't afford flying lessons so I went to Plan B. I got a job refueling and servicing light civilian aircraft at the local airport. At least I got to hang around airplanes. I also got to hang around two celebrities. Teamster Union boss Jimmy Hoffa was on trial in Chattanooga for jury tampering. He would fly in on Monday in a Twin Beechcraft with big radial engines and leave on Friday. At age 18, you're fearless but Hoffa brought guys with him that scared the shit out of me. His bodyguards were beefy men in dark suits and shades with bulges under their armpits and fierce expressions. All had names ending in vowels. They watched every move involving servicing the aircraft. Hoffa's caution was justified. The mob later whacked him.

On the other end of the spectrum was golfer Arnold Palmer. The Arnold Palmer golf equipment company was located in Chattanooga. He visited occasionally, personally piloting his own Aero Commander twin. Palmer was a nice guy, the direct opposite of Hoffa, who definitely wasn't. We developed a first-name relationship. Arnold called me "Eddie" and I addressed him as "Mr. Palmer." Despite all this, I still looked forward to flying for the USAF, not pumping gas into Cessnas for a living.

However, if a military career didn't work out, I was mentally prepared to fly for the airlines instead. That would have been better than holding down a real job involving real work. Three years of Junior Reserve Officers Training Corps (JROTC) at Chattanooga High School followed by four years of USAF ROTC in college were stepping stones to the freedom of the wild blue yonder, to mix metaphors. In case I couldn't pass the flight physical, only three percent of young people in the USA can pass an entry-level military pilot's physical, I earned a degree in Mechanical Engineering. This allowed me to work as a designer for the Piper Aircraft Company in Vero Beach, FL while awaiting induction into active duty with the USAF. I also did some reliability test-flying for Piper.

The summer after my junior year in college at Georgia Tech, I spent six weeks undergoing basic officer training at Langley Air Force Base in tidewater Virginia. There I perfected my marching skills, polished my saluting régime, got a skin-head haircut, and learned how to make a bed with squared-away folded sheet corners. All were useful skills for a future fighter pilot, or so they told me.

Our unit at "summer camp" included a contingent of officer candidates from Howard University in Washington, DC, an all-Black school. Growing up in the then-segregated South, in New Orleans and Chattanooga, I had never sat down and enjoyed a conversation with a Black person. When I did so at Langley AFB, the experience was illuminating, probably the most useful time I spent while at camp. The verbal sessions we engaged in were more rewarding than learning how to roll socks into balls with little smiles on the folds. I like to think the Black guys got something worthwhile out of our bull-shooting sessions with me as well.

One fun thing we did was an introduction to survival training in the Great Dismal Swamp of Virginia. Whatever mental images are summoned by the moniker "Great Dismal Swamp" would be accurate. It was miserable. Standing outside a tent late one night, I heard several guys from Howard, all urban Blacks, talking. They had never been this close to raw nature. One spoke up:

"Cobleigh, that redneck, has been camping, hunting, and fishing all his life, stick close to him, he'll know what to do."

In return for my woodcraft, or rather Louisiana swamp knowledge, the Black guys introduced me to the best nightclub in Virginia Beach, VA. We took in all three shows put on by the Drifters, a Do-Wop Black group. They were great.

No Black guy in my basic training squadron aspired to be an aviator. They were dedicated to becoming Air Force officers, but not in flying billets. Why? I never found out. This sad situation continues today. At present only about 2% of USAF pilots are Black, for a total of about 50. Minorities don't seem to be attracted to flying, which is a shame. Our country needs as many gung-ho flyers as it can get. Also, advancement in the Air Force is heavily dependent on having silver wings on your chest. Back then, the idea that women could also be military aviators was absurd. That mistaken concept has been updated over the years. Now females fly, fight, and sometimes die for their country. Which is as it should be.

All this military preparation led me to Webb AFB, Texas for Undergraduate Pilot Training (UPT), class number 68B. Our class nickname was the "Green Hornets." When I reported on base for active duty, it was the beginning of a dream, a quest with a chance of being completed. But first things first. I needed to acquire a call sign.

A pilot's call sign is his or her nickname, one the aviator goes by in informal settings, such as with the squadron or at the bar. Sometimes it's painted on an aircraft under the canopy rail. Call signs are assigned by squadron mates, never by the individual in question. Indeed, any objection to a particular call sign is a sure way to make it permanent. I once was squadron mates with a Bill Higginbotham. He kept referring to himself as, and demanding people call him, "Wild Bill." Naturally, his call sign was "Higgy" assigned by the Squadron Commander himself. Call signs can change from squadron to squadron and as an aviator moves up the rank ladder. They are usually based on a physical characteristic, "Slim" for a muscular guy, or a play on a name, "Dusty" Rhodes, or "Bug" Roach, or an embarrassing mishap. Now with the welcome inclusion of women in squadrons, call signs tend to be in good taste. No longer will a well-hung guy be known as "Tripod."

After one stressful week of UPT, several of us unmarried guys visited a local bar and grill in Big Spring to down some burgers and sip a few adult beverages. The joint boasted a pool table. One pool game is called "Eight Ball" which anyone can play. Several matches took place with financial speculation on the outcomes. For some reason, I enjoyed the best night on a pool table I ever had, before or since.

Monday morning, my call sign was "Fast Eddie" after the pool shark, Fast Eddie Felton, played by Paul Newman in the film *The Hustler*. My friend Rich Long came up with the moniker. I pretended to object, which instantly welded the new call sign in place. While the guys referenced the movie's fictional protagonist, I knew the original "Fast Eddie" was Captain Eddie Rickenbacker, the USA's ace-of-aces in WWI and the Commander of the 27th Aero fighter squadron, the famous "Hat-In-The-Ring" outfit. He brought the nickname with him into the US Army Air Corps. Rickenbacker earned it as a racing driver competing in the Indianapolis 500 before The Great War. Having the same call sign as Rickenbacker, an aviation legend, was super cool. Somehow it stuck throughout my USAF career. Even today, over 50 years later, I get emails addressed to "Fast Eddie." My wife, Heidi, and I have a nine-foot tournament pool table in our basement game room where she regularly beats me like a drum at Eight Ball.

Initial flight training at UPT was inflicted by the T-41 Mescalero, a stripped-down, militarized version of the Cessna 172, a propeller-driven, tricycle landing gear, light plane. Such craft spend all their flight hours at low level among swarms of insects. The resulting mess smeared on the wings' leading edges and the windshield earned the bird the title of "Bug Smasher." Still, the T-41 sported "United States Air Force" and the USAF emblem painted on its faded aluminum skin. I got to fly a military aircraft as an almost-military pilot. The T-41 cruised at about 120 mph. It could barely kill me.

Thanks to AFROTC, I already won my Private Pilot license. That, coupled with my experience with Piper Aircraft, made flying the T-41 a piece of cake. Or so I thought. The T-41 was jeered at as the "propeller-driven washing machine." Its mission was to weed out, to "wash out," guys who were unsuited to being USAF pilots for any reason, including cockiness. The instructor pilots, the IPs, were charged with ensuring the flying was conducted in the USAF way, no matter what the fledgling pilots thought about the exact process.

On my T-41 check ride, the Instructor Pilot, the IP, asked, "What would you do to abort a take-off?"

The proper response was to parrot verbatim the standard, published, bold-faced procedure, "**THROTTLE CLOSE. BRAKES APPLY.**"

My answer, "Chop the throttle and stand on the brakes."

"You didn't give me the bold face procedure," the IP replied.

"You didn't ask me for the procedure, you asked me what I would do."

Things went downhill from there. He even dinged me on the knots I used to tie down the aircraft after the busted check ride. I used a sheepshank knot which allows adjustment of tension without untying the hold-down rope. He wanted a dumb-assed double hitch which results in a slack tie-down.

I got the message. For my re-check, potentially my last flight in the USAF, I mouthed the right words and tied the correct knots.

No one in our UPT class washed out in the T-41, despite my best efforts to do so. The class ahead of us had one guy who threw up on his first two flights. Airsickness can be overcome with practice, but this poor soul vomited while walking out to the aircraft for his elimination check ride. He was dismissed with a MOA label, Manifestations Of Apprehension, or fear of flying. Not to be confused with the book, *Fear of Flying*, by Erica Jong with the same name but definitely not the same theme. What did the washed-out soul's fear spring from, being suspended in mid-air in a flimsy airplane held aloft by obscure principles of aerodynamics? Maybe he worried about entering the military aviator's domain. With brushfire wars burning in the Middle East and Southeast Asia, the danger to a USAF pilot's life and limbs were readily apparent to all. Another guy washed out due to a lack of aptitude. He grew up in New York City. The only mechanical conveyance he ever operated was an elevator. He couldn't drive a car.

T-41 training was conducted mostly by civilians at the Howard County airport, a civilian field just north of Big Spring. The airport hosted light planes and regular flights by Trans Texas Airlines, or TTA, a.k.a Tree Top Airlines. TTA flew WWII surplus DC-3's but had cute flight attendants who never over-nighted in Big Spring. Pity. Howard County didn't fit my image of a USAF base but it was a first baby step.

After my adventures in the T-41, bigger and better aircraft, i.e., jets, awaited on the Webb AFB flight line. Our class began flying the T-37 basic trainer, none too soon. I could hardly wait.

CHAPTER TWO
UNDERGRADUATE PILOT TRAINING II

Tweety-Birds and Talons

The T-37 trainer was one of the few military jets not requiring a boarding ladder or external steps to mount and enter the cockpit. It crouched low to the tarmac. You just walked up and climbed in like Burt Reynolds jumping into his black Pontiac Trans Am through the open T-tops, only without a screaming chicken decal on the hood. Once tightly strapped in the ejection seat, which the Trans Am lacked, you were confronted with a proper instrument panel festooned with multiple switches, gauges, levers, and dials. It looked like a real airplane while the T-41's panel resembled the dashboard of a Studebaker pick-up truck without the steering column-mounted gear shift lever and knob.

The T-37 was propelled, slowly, by two tiny J-69 jet engines making just over 1000 pounds of thrust each. The J-69's radial compressor section, which fed high-pressure air to the combustion chambers, used the same mechanical configuration as the old hand-cranked sirens mounted on vintage fire trucks. The result was the same, a high-pitched scream. The USAF hesitated in giving the T-37 an official nickname, so its pilots attached one, the "Tweety-Bird" or just the "Tweet." Why? The diminutive jet sounded like the world's loudest dog whistle.

The Tweet was a miserable beast to fly, noisy, hot (no cabin pressurization or A/C), under-powered, and slow. Worst of all was the side-by-side seating arrangement with the IP on the right, the student on the left. The USAF Air Training Command (ATC) somehow adopted the notion of that having the IP in such close proximity to the student would somehow enhance the quality of instruction. Maybe so, but that configuration meant the junior birdman didn't sit on the aircraft's centerline. This skewed the view seen out the windscreen. The offset

AND I LIVED TO TELL THE TALES

angle required a mental adjustment to the correct picture of the aircraft's attitude during aerobatic maneuvers. Still, when I went on my first solo flight in the Tweet, I looked to my right to make sure I was truly alone. Then I looked down at my leather-gloved hands on the stick and throttles. I could hardly believe I was flying a jet aircraft all by myself, albeit slowly.

In later years, the USAF planned to replace the Tweety-Bird with the T-46 Next Generation Trainer, NGT, which also featured side-by-side seating for the student and the instructor. When asked why they continued this set-up, instead of using tandem seating as flown by every other basic jet trainer in the world, Air Training Command's spokesperson replied "If tandem seating was superior, we would already be using it." The mind boggles at the follies of officialdom. The T-46 NGT was cancelled due to murky politics and a budget crunch. It took Republic Aviation with it into bankruptcy after only three test aircraft were built. Much later, the USAF finally came to its collective senses, replacing the Tweet with the T-6A Texan II, a turboprop which sports proper tandem seating. The T-6A has about the same performance as the legendary P-51 Mustang fighter of WWII, which it resembles in flight, a graphic indication of aeronautical progress.

The T-37 was the last USAF jet that could enter a spin on purpose and recover. A spin is the only aerodynamically stable maneuver. No pilot input is needed to maintain it. Every other trick an aircraft can perform requires a pilot active on the controls. In a spin, it was great fun watching the world seemingly rotate around, rushing up to meet the Tweet's cockpit. Unless the stick and rudder were manipulated correctly, the aircraft would have continued to spin until impact. Fortunately, the spin recovery procedure was simple, only 37 bold-faced words in the manual, and effective.

Only IPs flying with other IPs were allowed to perform an inverted spin. Much later, I flew a Jet Provost trainer with the Royal Air Force. That craft looked like a giant, single-engine Tweet. You could spin inverted in the Jet Provost. Once was enough.

The Tweet with all its flaws reached, just barely, jet speeds. It also involved jet levels of danger, a fact I knew then intellectually but not emotionally, at least not at first.

It was mid-afternoon when we got word that John Dalke and his instructor pilot were dead. They took off early in the morning in a T-37 on a routine instructional flight over the wastelands west of the air base, between Big Spring and Midland. When they didn't return and once their maximum fuel-limited flight time expired, the Base Operations troops began calling all the local airfields in case the duo landed off base after an inflight emergency. No success. There was still hope they could have landed at one of the many private, uncontrolled airfields, or crop duster bases, or dirt ranch strips, bladed out of the mesquite tree-infested landscape. Many of these were scattered throughout Texas's parched plains. Or the pair, both United States Air Force officers, could have ejected from a jet in serious trouble, such as an inflight fire or a control system malfunction. They might have been walking to a road leaving their parachutes behind. No luck on this scenario either.

Around noon, a phone call came in to the base switchboard. It was immediately transferred to the Base Operations Flight Safety office. A water pump technician was on the other end of the land line speaking with a classic West Texas drawl. He had been repairing a windmill which drove a well pump replenishing a watering trough for free-ranging cattle. From his perch at the top of the windmill tower, maybe fifty feet in the air, he observed a tiny jet plane screaming like a banshee, skimming across the semi-desert landscape at very low attitude. The mechanic later stated he thought the aircraft was below him, which would have been very unlikely but not impossible. He watched as the jet pulled up into the beginning of a loop, tucked under inverted at the loop's apex, then begin to pull out the dive at the bottom of the vertical circle. They almost made it. The crash tore through the scrubby mesquite trees throwing branches and shooting flames into the dry air as the plane smeared itself and its pilots across the ground. It came to rest at last, starting a small brush fire. A loop is an altitude-losing maneuver in a T-37, the end of the loop is always lower than the starting point. If a loop is begun down on the deck, chances of recovering before impact are close to zero.

John Dalke was a gregarious sort of guy, always ready to share a drink or a story at the Officer's Club bar. On weekends, he would hang out there, hoping to shoot the bull with some of the F-104 pilots stationed at Webb AFB in a fighter-interceptor squadron of the USAF Air Defense Command, ADC. What the short-ranged Starfighter was defending in Texas and who the invaders would be wasn't clear. Perhaps heavy bombers from Mexico, or New Mexico. But there they were, flying the Mach Two, stubby winged "missile with a man in it" with its howling J-79 afterburning engine. Most of us pilot trainees considered the F-104 jocks to be demi-gods. We couldn't hope to rub elbows with such men. But not Dalke, he chatted them up.

Dalke's instructor cultivated a reputation as a wild hare. Late on Fridays, he was known to land, turn off the runway, and begin taxing back to the ramp. The control tower at Webb was at the far north end of the airfield, the runways ran far south. The taxi back, along 7500 feet of asphalt, took forever when Happy Hour beckoned. The approved taxi speed was limited to "a fast-walking pace" according to the ATC manuals. The IP, once out of sight of the tower, would jam the throttles forward, take off, get airborne, and fly most of the length of the taxiway ten feet in the air, touch down lightly, hit the brakes, then turn off onto the parking ramp as if nothing untoward had occurred. Evidently, this blatant disregard for safety regulations and obvious distain for the laws of aerodynamics cost us student pilots of Class 68B our new-found friend. A pair of parents lost their sons. This fatal crash brought home to me the fact that flying is inherently hazardous. This concept I had accepted in the abstract, but not personally, until then, until there was a vacant stool at the bar. Not until a USAF sergeant carefully packed up someone's belongings to ship home to his next of kin. John Dalke was the first person I ever knew who was killed in a plane crash. He wouldn't be the last.

Before joining the USAF, I lost a high school friend. He was electrocuted when a high-voltage power line fell on the metal farm shed where he was working. In college, a fraternity brother spun his car on a rain-slickened Atlanta freeway. He fell out, no seat belts, was run over and killed. These losses were random events, the black swans, or more accurately, the ravens, of mortality. Such events can't be predicted, nor easily prevented, nor mentally prepared for. In pilot training, I was immersed in a new military world where violent death was a common occurrence. Where the chances of cashing in my chips were ever-present, part of the job description. That was new. Looking back, I wonder if I had known what was in store along the path I chose, would I have done anything differently. In South East Asia during the Vietnam War, my squadron lost one in seven souls. I concluded later in life if I had glimpsed the future, I would have done the same damn things. When 23 years old, you think yourself to be invulnerable, immortal. That attitude is what allows wars, mainly conducted by young people, to be fought.

Later that afternoon, I called my own parents back in East Tennessee to reassure them. If they saw something in the news about a fatal USAF crash in West Texas, it wasn't me. They hadn't heard a thing. Numerous US Air Force pilot training bases were scattered across the South and Southwest. A smaller number of US Navy bases fledged Naval Aviators. Various US Army helicopter training posts whirled away. The loss of just two pilots at an obscure base in West Texas didn't merit a line of ink in the newspapers nor a mention on the six o'clock TV news. Aerial sudden death sadly became routine, another sense of perspective I reluctantly hoisted aboard.

After the accident investigation concluded, I salvaged the wreck of the T-37 and removed one of the control stick grips. Then, all USAF jets used a standard black stick grip festooned with an array of red buttons and an honest-to-God trigger, also red. On the Tweet, none of the buttons, especially the trigger, worked except for the radio transmit button. Fabricating an adapter, I replaced the gear shift lever knob on my Corvette with the USAF stick grip. My intention was to wire the unit to operate the turn signals, lights, horn etc. After only a week, I removed it, replacing it with the standard Chevy chromed ball that came with the car.

My girlfriend at the time was a pretty, smart, blond Texan from Big Spring with big hair. Donna had a great ass, silky-smooth skin, and an aversion to wearing panties. She asked why I replaced the original shift knob, liking the aircraft-based unit. My answer was the stick grip was too heavy, making the shift linkage rattle. That was true, but it was not the real reason. It creeped me out knowing the last hand to touch that particular grip was now on a dead man.

Once my sojourn in the T-37 Tweety-Bird mercifully ended, my class and I transitioned into the T-38 Talon advanced trainer.

The T-38 was, and still is, a real jet, modified from the F-5 Freedom Fighter, a (very) light jet fighter intended for sale to lower-end allied air forces. The Talon got its nickname from the shape of its fuselage, resembling the talon of a bird of prey, a raptor's claw. We called it the "White Rocket." It was fast, supersonic when called upon to be so. With tandem seating, the student enjoyed an unobstructed view out the windscreen on the aircraft's centerline while the poor IP was forced to peer around the student's ejection seat from his own position low in the rear cockpit. I loved it. I took to the White Rocket and was the first of my class to go solo in it. This feat of aerial expertise got me chucked by my mates into a stock tank full of dirty water placed in front of the squadron building for just such juvenile antics. I didn't mind a bit.

Flight training in the T-38 was super fun. Solo, you could make yourself believe you were piloting a supersonic fighter. The aircraft handled well. It felt light on the controls and showed no obvious vices. You couldn't spin it. It was almost too good, requiring no rudder input to coordinate turns. In most other airplanes, you bank with the ailerons and coordinate the turn with the rudder pedals. In the T-38, you could fly a mission with your feet flat on the cockpit floor. This generated a bad habit I later had to un-learn. Afterburner thrust was just a throttle push away. If I left the engines in afterburner, Mach One, the "sound barrier," waited in front of the needle nose.

We were supposed to file a report every time we went supersonic in case any citizen of the West Texas complained, which they never did. I strongly suspect more sonic booms happened than reports were inked. Roll rate in a T-38 was 720 degrees-a-second. If you shoved the control stick full left or right, the sky was replaced by the ground in the canopy above you. The sky came back around twice in one second. You can't do that even in an F-104. I know, I tried later. But, aileron rolls were the only thing more fun in a T-38 than a Starfighter. During my scheduled solo flights, I was supposed to practice maneuvers for upcoming check rides. I probably would have scored higher on the resulting grade sheets if I had actually done the practice instead of just........flying for the sheer joy of it.

The most difficult task in flying the T-38, other than wiping the grin, under your oxygen mask, off your face, was landing it. In the traffic pattern, you flew downwind, parallel to the runway and offset from it. At a certain point, you rolled into a 180-degree descending turn, ideally with the landing gear down and locked. The objective was to roll out on short final approach lined up with the runway and at the right airspeed. This maneuver required the aircraft to achieve several conflicting objectives: lose altitude, slow down, and turn tightly. The only indication that you were doing it right was the airspeed indicator providing, a second-order, indirect input.

The prime directive in landing the White Rocket was to not stall in the final turn. A stall occurs when the Angle of Attack, the AOA, is too high. This is the angle at which the airflow encounters the wings. Too much AOA and the wing stalls, the airflow separates into random turbulence, all lift is lost, and a spin-crash-and-burn accident results. However, indicated airspeed is a poor means of monitoring AOA.

The USN Navy possesses considerable experience in landing airplanes on boats. Personally, I think aircraft carrier operations fall under Article 140 of the Uniform Code of Military Justice, Un-Natural Acts, but the Navy does it well. To land with precision, as in the USN, requires an AOA gauge. Wings stall on AOA and nothing else. Now, all aircraft have AOA gauges, making landings a piece of cake, unless you are doing it on a boat.

An objective of the T-38 landing drills, other than not crashing, was to fly a tight final turn. Too big a pattern wastes fuel, wastes time, and looks like the pilot is inept. A measure of a good turn onto final was the Big Spring Holiday Inn. Your turn needed to be executed before passing over the motel. If the Holiday Inn was visible inside of the turn, you were too wide. My IP had a wry way of telling me to tighten up.

He would say, looking down at the inside of my turn to final, "Wow, look at all those girls at the Holiday Inn pool."

When things got really loose, I heard, "Ed, do you have the airfield in sight?"

As a result of all this subtle prodding, I learned well. Throughout my USAF flying career, I was known for flying tight patterns whether in the traffic pattern or on the gunnery range.

One training requirement involved a weekend cross-country flight with your IP and one other T-38 in formation. We took off from Webb AFB after duty on a Friday and landed in Albuquerque, NM after dark. Kirtland AFB shares an airfield with the city's big international airport and is located near downtown. Landing there with sparkling city lights all around and airliners coming and going was like being called up to the major leagues from a minor league baseball team and finding yourself in Yankee Stadium. Was I stoked? You bet. The next day, we flew on to Las Vegas and then Peterson Field outside of Colorado Springs, CO. As in Albuquerque, Peterson Field is dual-use; many civilian planes operate out of there. As our flight of two took the runway leaving "C-Springs," I heard the control tower transmit on the radio to another aircraft, a bug smasher.

"Cessna 75 Juliet, use caution. Air Force jet fighters on takeoff roll."

I asked the IP in the rear cockpit, "Jet fighters? Where?"

The answer came back in my earphones, "That's us, you moron."

However, not everyone in our class was a moron, probably just me. We were a diverse, if White, group and that was a good thing. I got to know, well, guys from all over the country and from different backgrounds.

CHAPTER THREE
WEBB AFB, 1966-1967

The Fearless Flyers of Class 68B

The junior birdmen of Class 68B were educationally and culturally a mixed lot. Out of the 55 students, about half were recent graduates of the US Air Force Academy, the USAFA. Another 30% were commissioned through the AFROTC program from civilian colleges or universities. The rest came to us courtesy of Officer Candidate School, OCS.

The USAFA Second Lieutenants were referred to as "Zoomies" from their own name for their alma mater, the "Zoom School." They had been through a four- or five-year intensive program similar, some would say way too similar, to those at the US Army's West Point and the US Navy's Annapolis service academies. There are those of us who had hoped the USAF would have structured a more liberal educational institution instead of replicating 200+ years of mindless military tradition. At other UPT bases, particularly Williams AFB outside Phoenix AZ, Zoomies gained a bad reputation for having an entitlement attitude. Conventional wisdom at Williams held they all had been brainwashed into thinking that, due to their superior military education, each and every one was destined to be Chief of Staff of the USAF or at least to be a General Officer. They were perceived as thinking the AFROTC and OCS officers in their UPT classes were doomed to be USAF career flunky-butts.

I didn't see any of this at Webb. The Zoomies of 68B fit right in, no untoward arrogance was ever apparent to me. All of us, regardless of our origins, were of equal status. The only difference I noted was the Academy graduates showed a little more dedication to continuing a career as a USAF officer regardless of eventual flying status and less of a tendency to view UPT as a stepping stone to the pay, status, and monetary rewards of an airline pilot. No matter, we all got along, no one looked down on anyone else. We were all equally challenged and humbled by the intense UPT experience.

Back then, all of us were White males. Few Blacks attended pilot training in the 1960's for whatever reasons. The inclusion of female pilots wasn't even on the distant horizon, which in flat West Texas is very distant indeed. As noted, many women are now military pilots, but Blacks are still absent from cockpits in great numbers. This is a shame, as a military force in a democracy should approximate the ethnic make-up of the general population. But more importantly, a country's military prowess is greatly influenced by the number and quality of its service pilots. Excluding 13% of the candidates by race reduces the available pool of talent. Today, the Chief of Staff of the USAF is a Black man, General C.Q. Brown Jr., an F-16 pilot. Maybe his example will bring more volunteers from the Black community to UPT in the future.

If there was anyone who was humbled by the UPT experience, it was EJ Dymer. EJ came from the AFROTC unit at the University of Pittsburgh where he was a BMOC, Big Man On Campus, the President of his fraternity, and quite the ladies' man, according to Dymer. He was an outgoing, friendly type, an unmarried person with many friends. Evidently he expected to continue his college successes at UPT. This came to a crashing halt when in the altitude chamber. He put his flight helmet on backwards. The altitude chamber was a submarine-like windowed tank from which the most of the air could be pumped out. The chamber trained us on the physiological effects of high altitude and of oxygen deprivation. Wearing your helmet backwards wasn't the way to go. Compounding matters, Dymer later in the same chamber put his vital oxygen mask on upside down with the hose pointing slightly upward. These were legendary screw-ups. Word spread rapidly throughout the base community and hapless EJ became known as the guy who wore his flight gear backwards and inverted. He tried without success to live down the humiliation. I suspect EJ never recovered confidence in himself and as a result his performance in UPT suffered for it. At the end of pilot training, EJ was assigned to fly the B-52 Stratofortress heavy bomber instead of the fighter plane he envisioned. Disappointed, he visited the US Navy recruiter in Big Spring inquiring about transferring to the Navy. That didn't work either. I have to say EJ never lost his sense of humor or his good spirits. Sociologists tell us that about one-half of our life's happiness is due to genetics. EJ had good genes.

Every four students were assigned to each IP. We all sat around in the crew room, four to a government-issued grey metal table, when not flying. When ground-bound and just sitting there, we were supposed to study for our next training mission or for our next ground school class. I am sure some studying occurred but I can't remember when it did. The lead IP, a Major continually urged our class Commander, Captain Ron Kautz, to, "Make these numbs look busy!" Ron, a grizzled veteran at age 27, tried.

Our class was comprised of all volunteers, no one ever gets drafted for pilot training. Likewise, no one volunteers for USAF, or USN, pilot training who is looking for a relaxed, or long, life. Tension was inevitable within the class. We were all competing with each other for class ranking which would determine our follow-on assignments. Type A personalities abounded in 68B, peopled with guys with records of achievement. Yet, we were expected to cooperate and do things as a class. It was a wonder we got along so well and continue to do so today.

Many folks smoked back then and EJ Dymer smoked menthol cigarettes constantly. Once when he was out flying, we cut a rubber band into an inch-long strip and shoved it with a toothpick into the next smoke in his pack, which he left lying on the table. We expected him to light up and instantly smell burning rubber. He smoked the whole butt and never noticed anything amiss. EJ Dymer passed away in 2012 of lung cancer. I often wondered if inhaling smoldering rubber contributed to his early demise. But not all our classmates came from the USAFA, OCS, or ROTC.

Three of our fellow students were from Iran. For some time, the US government had, in a low-key, under-the-radar program, trained Iranian pilots for the Shah of Iran's Imperial Iranian Air Force. Being chosen for flight training in the USA was, I later found out, quite a coup for a young Persian man. Sadly, the candidates were selected based on family connections, politics, or status, instead of potential aviation ability. Two of the Iranians were indifferent pilots, even when given extra chances to pass not afforded to Americans. One washed out and seemed relieved to be going home. The third, Jalal Payami, was different. He loved to fly and he was good at it.

As is the custom in USAF squadrons, good-natured kidding was incessant. We called the Persians "Camel Drivers" despite their protestations that they had never seen a camel in Iran, much less driven one. Jalal's call sign was "Black Camel" due to his dark hair and swarthy complexion. The Iranians, semi-devout Muslims, never frequented the Officer's Club bar, being teetotalers. However, the allure and accessibility of American women didn't escape their notice. In my not-so-humble opinion, Iran boasts the best-looking women in the world, but they are mostly unavailable at home due to the strict Islamic rules enforced there on the separation of sexes, not to mention the Muslim/Persian obsession with virginity. In later years, I spent two summers in an Iranian fighter squadron where I gained a keen appreciation for the Persian people and their ancient culture, notwithstanding the religious/political lunacy prevalent there today. More later on this.

The West Texas town of Big Spring was remote, half a day's drive from anywhere anyone had ever heard of. The town wasn't rich compared to the nearby twin oil boom cities of Midland, and Odessa to the west, but it was prosperous. Oil, farming, ranching, and the air base with its 2000 jobs drove the local economy. There were three, count 'em three, Wagon Wheel drive-in restaurants/singles bars.

One salient feature of Big Spring was the place was over-populated by Texans. They were everywhere with their big hats, big accents, and big smiles. The locals welcomed the GIs of Webb AFB with open arms, free Bar-B-Ques, and friendly support. Some of the local young women, Texas beauties all, were very friendly. Many an airman found a wife, a lover, or a mistress in Big Spring. I know I did. But that is another story. UPT classmate Mike Conners remembers the Mayor of Big Spring, who would meet and greet each incoming UPT class at a welcoming Bar-B-Que put on by the local Chevy dealer. His Honor told Mike, "You will have to drive 200 miles in any direction to have more fun than you can here in Big Spring." Well, maybe.

One place airmen weren't welcomed by the locals was the roadhouse and honky-tonk, called "The Stampede." Nightly, the house band, Hoyle Nix and His West Texas Cowboys, played their gigs behind a chicken wire cage protecting the musicians from flying beer bottles. Hoyle Nix, and later his son Jody, were touted as the world's only left-handed fiddle players. So now you know. The Stampede was off limits to Air Force personnel. Few missed it. The base Officer's Club, NCO Club, and Airman's Club were congenial, cheap, and much safer, no chicken wire needed for a band.

While remote and isolated, Webb AFB wasn't the end of the world. That would have been Laredo AFB and Del Rio AFB, south on the Mexican border. Those two bases were the USAF's versions of Fort

Zinderneuf of French Foreign Legion fictional fame (catch the movie or read the book). At last, at the end of the "Fifty-Three Week Year," pilot training took 53 weeks, graduation from UPT and departure from Big Spring beckoned.

Before I left Big Spring, I scratched a mental ich. From the Webb traffic pattern, I spotted an oil drilling rig in the scrub desert near the field. One Saturday, I drove out to the site and asked the guys working there if I could check out the drilling rig. They welcomed me to climb up to the drill deck. Wearing hard hats, safety goggles, stiff leather gloves, and steel toed boots, they were dressed for success, or rather for safety. I, on the other hand, sported sneakers, jeans, tee shirt, and a baseball hat. This was in the days before OSHA.

The roughnecks, and yes that's an official labor term, showed me around the rig explaining how they drilled for oil. It was fascinating but they kept changing the subject and asking me what it was like to fly the jet planes they saw every day in the sky over their job site. The crew was in the process of changing the drill bit, pulling all the drill pipe out of the well. When the bit emerged, they wrenched it off and installed a new one, reversing the vertical pipe parade. The rotary, diamond-tipped oil well drill bit was invented by Howard Hughes's father. It was the foundation product of the Hughes Tool Company in Houston.

Hughes Tool, immensely profitable, served as the financial flywheel for Howard Hughes's empire of airlines, airplanes, movies, Hughes Aircraft, Hughes Helicopters, and his Las Vegas hotels/casinos, smoothing out the cash flow. I didn't know it at the time, but this was the beginning of several encounters I would have with the Hughes complex. The straw boss on the rig showed me the used-up bit. It was about the size of a waste basket and weighed 30-40 pounds. He told me he was supposed to turn it in to prove he had used it, but that no one every checked. Winking, he tossed the bit over the side of the rig. It thudded down in the sand near, but not on, my Corvette. When I left, I took the bit with me. It made a great doorstop in the BOQ. I did try to tell the oil rig guys what it was like to fly the T-38.

Recently, the USAF has seen fit to replace the 50+-year-old T-38, which, despite being upgraded into the T-38C with a more modern cockpit and HUD, is wearing out under decades of abuse by ham-fisted student pilots. The new jet is the T-7A "Red Hawk," so-named to honor the famous all-Black fighter wing of WWII, the "Red Tails." These renowned "Tuskegee Airmen" painted the tails of their P-51D Mustangs bright red in racial and unit pride. The T-7A has tandem seating. In fact, it has what the boffins of the development community call "stadium seating" where the IP sits higher in the rear cockpit than the student in front. This innovation gives the IP a much clearer view of the aerial action. The smart betting is the T-7A Red Hawk will have red paint on its twin tails. Let's hope it attracts more Black pilots.

Assignment for newly-minted pilots meant being selected to fly operational USAF aircraft (Unless a graduate was be sent to IP school as a "Plow Back" and returned to the Air Training Command). But before we could move on to the "real Air Force" we needed to put in the required flight time of 120 hours in the T-38 White Rocket. I had completed the last check ride and had worn out the syllabus but I was still three hours short as were several others. We had to burn up those hours, and jet fuel, or there existed a danger the ATC staffers would cut back the fuel and flight time allotment for subsequent classes. Instead of doing more advanced flight training such as tactical formation flying, Air Combat Maneuvers, ACM, or logging more much-needed instrument time, we were told to take off and orbit the field at high altitude in extended race-track patterns to stretch flight endurance until we logged the required hours. Your tax dollars at work.

Our assignments came through and I was destined to train as a fighter pilot, albeit in the rear cockpit of the two s-at F-4 Phantom II, sort of like being a fighter co-pilot, a previously unknown profession. Several of our jocks were sent to be F-100 pilots. The F-100 Super Sabre was a single-seat, single-engine fighter developed shortly after the Korean War. It was my first choice. I was slightly bummed not to get it, but not overly so. It would have been cool to fly a fighter all by myself, but I was going to the world's most advanced fighter jet of the time instead of a plane even then rapidly becoming obsolete. As events later unfolded, going to the F-4 was the best thing that could have happened to me. More on that adventure later.

Assignments varied. The guys aiming for an airline career selected and were awarded seats in the KC-135 Stratotanker the military version of the Boeing 707 airliner and a four-engine air refueling behemoth. Some opted for the C-141 Starlifter, a large transport aircraft. Others went to B-52's and the C-47 Skytrain, better known as the "Gooney Bird." The C-47 was a twin-engine, propeller-driven WWII light transport, a military version of the pre-WWII DC-3 airliner, with radial piston engines. It was deployed in the rapidly expanding war in Vietnam as a cargo plane which could get into rough-hewn, primitive airstrips.

My good friend Al Franci got a C-47 slot. During conversion training in Florida, he came to the conclusion that the Vietnam war was unwinnable as currently being fought, was immoral, and probably was illegal with no declaration of war being passed by Congress. He was right on at least two of those points. Al decided to apply for Conscientious Objector Status based on his opposition to the war. This would release him to civilian life and cancel any military obligations and/or benefits. But he didn't want anyone to think he was trying to get out of combat due to mere yellow cowardice. So, he flew a combat tour in South Vietnam for a year, getting shot at every day when it wasn't pouring down with monsoon rain. Then he applied for separation when he returned to the US. It was awarded with no hesitation. He had proved his personal point. Al spent some time flying bales of marijuana at low level, at night, in a twin-engine Beechcraft across the Mexican border to smuggler-operated air strips in the Texas and Arizona deserts. These flights were like a resupply mission to a Special Forces camp in the Vietnamese highlands only with the Good Guys, i.e. the law, shooting at him instead of the Bad Guys, i.e., the Viet Cong. I asked him why he eventually quit the gig. Was it the danger, the illegality, the shifty people he dealt with? He said he just got tired of wrestling heavy bales of weed into and out of the aircraft under pressure and in the dark. I think he just got tired of hauling around the bales of twenty-dollar bills he earned the hard way.

Before our class left Webb AFB, a few of us unhinged bachelor types, led by Al Franci, made a movie chronicling our time in UPT. We borrowed a 16mm movie camera from the base Photo Lab and scrounged some gun camera film from the F-104 squadron. I often wondered why all the gun camera footage I had ever seen was so lousy; grainy, high contrast, low resolution black and white images. I learned it was probably due to the negative film supplied to the US government by the lowest bidder. This worked out. Our graduation movie had the same look as the ol' timey newsreels shown at theatres before the main feature, the low-quality imagery lending an air of authenticity.

For a boffo ending to the 68B epic film, we built a bomb. We cut off red golf bag tubular inserts and taped them together to resemble sticks of dynamite. A large, manual alarm clock and a dry cell battery, all connected by loops of black wiring, and mounted on a short wooden plank completed the cartoon-like "bomb." We filmed a masked Al Franci placing the bomb in a cardboard box and leaving it in front of the Wing Commander's office door. The next scene pictured the WC, a full colonel, opening the box on his desk. Instead of an explosion, a hand came out of the box and smashed a custard pie into the colonel's surprised face.

The WC, Colonel Chester Butcher, was a good sport to go along with the gag. He later led an Air Commando wing in Thailand during the Vietnam War. Butcher earned a reputation for taking more risks in combat than many of his underlings, which is really saying something. But what would one expect from a commander who agrees to get creamed with a pie in the face by a bunch of junior officers?

I believe, based on zero evidence, that we were the first class to make a class movie. Now, with recording capability available on every smart phone, many UPT classes produce short videos of their adventures in pilot training. However, I seriously doubt pies-in-the-face are enshrined in these videos.

UPT class 68B was tight. Many of us keep in touch. We have reunions. One scribe, Ed Petersen, takes inputs and publishes a Christmas newsletter each year for those of us still on the right side of the daisies. I doubt the Williams AFB UPT classes do that. A few years ago, Tom Brandon, a classmate, and his wife came through our town, Paso Robles, CA. We got together an had a great time. My wife, Heidi, asked when we had last seen each other. The answer; 42 years ago. She was amazed that we could sync up after so long an interval. No problem.

When his stint in the training command ended, my T-37 Tweet IP left the Air Force and joined a country and western music band in Oklahoma. I never found out if a chicken wire protective cage was needed. Years later, I ran into my T-38 IP at the Officer's Club at Nellis AFB, in Las Vegas, NV. He recognized me instantly and his cheery greeting rang out along the bar, "Hey, you're still alive!" I took that as a vote of confidence.

However, the idyllic existence at UPT did come to an end. I reported for duty in "The Real Air Force" a mystical place which all the freshly-frocked pilots looked forward to. A war erupted in Southeast Asia in the early 1960's. North Vietnam intended to unite itself with South Vietnam by force if necessary. The whole peninsula was aflame with guerrilla warfare, armed insurrections, and violence. Air power would play a major role in that last dynamic. I was destined to participate in some way. But first, I needed to learn how to fly an actual fighter plane. I took down my black and white poster of Captain "Fast Eddie" Rickenbacker from the wall of my room in the Bachelor Officers Quarters, the BOQ, rolled it up, and reported to the Tactical Air Command.

Several years later, when I was stationed in Las Vegas, a real hardship posting, a friend and squadron mate, Hal Rhoden, and I flew an F-4 to Big Spring to re-visit our old stomping grounds. Hal had been an IP at Webb AFB.

The F-4 was originally designed to land on USN aircraft carriers. On a boat, the objective is to plant the airplane firmly on the deck in the landing zone to pick up an arresting cable. Thus, the Phantom could withstand quite a jolt on touchdown. Our USAF F-4s had different wheels, tires, and landing gear struts but could still take a licking on landing. In UPT, we were taught to gently settle the aircraft on the runway, to let it down easy. A good landing was one where you needed to call the mobile control tower to ask if you had touched down yet. "Mobile" was a short, small control tower stationed at each the end of the dual runways to monitor student landings.

On the Friday afternoon flight to Webb, Rhoden was in the front cockpit of the F-4. I was in the rear. I talked him into impressing the IPs and students stationed in Mobile with the F-4's ruggedness by executing a carrier-type landing. He plunked the bird down with a splat on the painted runway numbers just abeam mobile. Hal was good at that.

Sunday afternoon, we left Webb with me in the front cockpit and the future Brigadier General in the back seat. I request an unrestricted departure from the main control tower. Sunday afternoon with nothing going on; the controllers were only too happy to give permission. On take-off, I lifted off, sucked up the landing gear and wing flaps then held the aircraft down on the runway accelerating all the while. As the airspeed built rapidly and the aerodynamic trim altered, the nose wanted badly to come up. The F-4 acted like a real animal, not a phantom, eager to leap skyward. I could have rolled on nose-down trim to balance the stick forces, but at 100 feet altitude that idea didn't appeal to me.

At a UPT base, everyone monitors aircraft operations at all times. I was sure the F-4's unfamiliar J-79 engines, screaming in afterburner, would attract universal attention. We had achieved over 400 knots, 450 mph, by the end of the runway. Relaxing forward pressure on the stick, I let the nose climb to 60 degrees up which would appear to be straight up from the field. It certainly felt like straight up in the cockpit. The air-show-off departure was intended to give the Webb AFB UPT pogues something to aspire to, a demonstration of the Real Air Force. It was great juvenile fun. But, don't take it just from me. I asked one of our more distinguished, as opposed to extinguished, graduates to contribute to this book. His input is next.

Chapter Three B
A SIGNAL FROM THE HEAD SHED

My Days at Webb AFB

Thirty years in the Air Force and the year I most remember were those early days at Webb AFB. For me, these memories are as vivid today as they were some 55+ years ago, just arriving at Webb AFB in September 1966 and finding out I had my own bedroom with a shared bathroom after my prison-life days at VMI was like a gift from heaven.

Now, we all arrived at UPT with different flying backgrounds. Some had considerable flying experience, while others like myself, didn't know the difference between an aileron and rudder. I remember the challenges of trying to land a T-41 in the crosswinds of West Texas, my T-37 solo, and our T-38 solo night navigation flights to and from Amarillo AFB. We were lined up like ducks in a row, praying the lead aircraft with its flashing lights could find Big Spring. And then there were the week-end trips to Midland and our Friday-night gatherings at the Officers Club for Happy Hour. We also experience the potential dangers of flying with the tragic loss of our classmate, John Dalke.

We were fortunate to have strong leadership in our class with Brad Vansant and Ron Kautz, who kept us straight and taught us there were other important requirements to being an officer that extend well beyond the cockpit. Another special person in the life of our class was Cal Lowry. As Head of the UPT Athletic Program, Cal took a special interest in our class and will always be remembered with great affection for his encouragement and support.

After we graduated from UPT and received our Wings, we all went our separate ways. Some made the military a career while others completed their military commitment and entered public life. However, what we all have in common is that we honorably served our country in uniform and successfully completed UPT as proud members of Class 68-B Green Hornets.

Lawrence E. Boese
Lt. Gen. (Ret.), USAF

CHAPTER FOUR
DAVIS MONTHAN AFB, TUCSON, AZ, 1968

Ol' Double Ugly

The McDonnell F-4 Phantom II fighter plane reeked of ugliness, there wasn't any way around that esoteric judgement. It seemed to be a collection of odd angles with pieces attached at random locations and led by a bulbous black nose. Why? One might ask. The story begins with the US Navy.

In the early 1950's the Navy needed, according to the McDonnell Aircraft Company, a new fighter. The early generation of straight-wing, subsonic shipboard fighters were soon to be rendered obsolete by the march of aerodynamic progress. Replacements were in the pipeline for some naval flight missions but not all. The F-8 Crusader, with its four 20mm cannon, was the dogfighter of the future, should any dogfights break out, a possibility some "experts" considered unlikely. The A-4 Skyhawk would fill the light ground attack role. But what about defending the aircraft carrier? Russian bombers could stand off and launch missiles from out of range of the F-8 and in the weather or at night, thereby avoiding the F-8 Crusader, a day fighter with a small, range-limited radar set.

McDonnell convinced naval planners of the need for a longer-range, radar-equipped fighter which could intercept incoming Bad Guys and shoot down said enemy with all-weather, radar-guided missiles. The company's proposal was accepted despite McDonnell's checkered past at designing fighter aircraft. One McDonnell naval fighter was such a turkey the entire inventory of several dozen planes was grounded as unsafe to fly. They were floated on a barge from the factory in Saint Louis down the Mississippi River to a USN training base in Mississippi to serve as maintenance trainers.

The Phantom II sprang from the drawing boards and slide rules (no computers back then) of the McDonnell engineers, Construction of first prototypes was well under way. However, wind tunnel testing revealed several glaring defects promising unstable aerodynamics for the new bird. Rather than revise the existing design at great cost and time, the boffins tweaked the existing prototype aircraft to fix the problems. The wings tilted up 12 degrees at the wing-fold joint. The horizontal stabilators, the tailplanes, tilted down 23 degrees, sawtooth leading edges were added to the wings, and the gaping air intakes for the twin engines were offset out from the fuselage. The big black nose was needed to house a big radar antenna dish and could not be made sleeker or more pointed.

McDonnell used two J-79 afterburning engines for the Phantom. They had gained experience in twin-engined fighters with the F-101 VooDoo interceptor for the USAF which mounted two J-57 turbojets. The F-101 was another lemon of an airplane with the engines partially exposed to the airflow. They wouldn't fit inside. The "One-Oh-Wonder" had heavier wing loading than the iconic F-104 which mounted virtually no wings at all. This lack of fighter success by McDonnell Aircraft deterred no one in the decision process. The F-4 flew for the first time in 1958.

The aircraft was manned by two crew members, a pilot in the front cockpit and a Radar Intercept Officer, a RIO, in the rear. At least they used tandem seating. The RIO operated the powerful radar and the navigation set. Armament consisted of four AIM-7 Sparrow medium-range radar-guided missiles and four AIM-9 Sidewinder heat-seeking short-range missiles. No gun was installed. Tacticians thought one to be unnecessary, they believed all future air combat would be beyond bullet range, making guns passé. Besides, the only modern gun available was the M61 20mm Vulcan gatling gun developed for the F-104. The Naval Air Systems Command's grandees would rather collectively eat a bug than adopt a USAF gun system even if it did spit out 100 lethal rounds a second. Initial flight tests were successful and the Phantom was ordered into series production for the Navy.

Meanwhile, the USAF found itself in a similar fix as the Navy. During the 1950's, the Air Force was run totally by bomber pilots fixated on strategic bombing despite the lack of success in WWII. Pentagon planners, as usual, assumed the Russians were similarly obsessed. To maintain any sort of fighter force, the USAF tried to make its fighters as "strategic" as possible. Interceptors such as the F-102 Delta Dart, the F-

106 Delta Dagger, the F-104 Starfighter, and the F-101 VooDoo were designed, built, and deployed. The sole ground attack member of the Century Series fighters (so-named as all the ID number began with 100) was the F-105 Thunderchief fighter/bomber. It was designed to deliver a single nuclear bomb at high speed.

Slowly the light dawned in the basement of the Pentagon that the USAF had no long range, penetrating fighter capable of both air combat and counter-air operations. The legacy of the legendary P-51 Mustang of WWII had been squandered. Enter a bean-counting executive from the Ford Motor Company.

Robert McNamara was appointed by President Lyndon Johnson as his Secretary of Defense with the mission of introducing corporate efficiencies into the Department of Defense. With no extensive military background and no ability nor the inclination to learn from those around him who did possess tactical knowledge and military experience, McNamara set to work. Ignoring the obvious fact that the USN and USAF had very different missions and needs, he decreed, as the two services both flew fighters, they would fly the same fighters and tons of money would be saved by not developing a new bird for the USAF. The USAF would instead buy the Navy's F-4 Phantom reaping economies of scale in the resulting procurement contracts. In return, the USAF would develop the next generation multi-role fighter, which turned out to be the F-111 Aardvark, for both services. The ill-advised F-111 project was another disaster, one too long and sad to recount here.

Under orders from the Pentagon, the USAF set about converting the F-4 to its needs as best as possible. A full set of flight controls was added to the rear cockpit which would be occupied by pilots, like me, not RIOs, at least not initially. One could, and I did, fly the jet from the rear cockpit. Air Force aerial refueling gear was fitted along with ground-based landing gear and an inertial navigation set. The Navy possessed the foresight to fit seven hard points on the wings and fuselage for external fuel tanks and for air-to-ground ordinance so that requirement was already filled. The aircraft was already configured to carry the AIM-7 Sparrow radar-guided missiles semi-submerged in the belly. The Air Force development community ate their own symbolic bug and bought the Sparrow. However, they drew the turf line at the AIM-9 Sidewinder, requiring the jet to use the AIM-4 Falcon short range, heat-seeking missile. The Hughes Aircraft Company designed the Falcon to shoot down bombers flying straight and level, not for dogfighting with the Bad Guys' fighters.

It was also intended for internal carriage on the F-102 and F-106 interceptors and not to be hung out in the airflow and in the weather while exposed on a wing pylon. But hey, it was a USAF missile. Compounding the USN's mistake, no gun was installed. A later version, the F-4E, mounted the M61 gun when USAF fighter pilots threatened to mutiny after being sent out onto the notional streets of Dodge City with empty holsters.

The Navy F-4's with their dull grey paint scheme had a sort of flying domestic appliance look to them which was passable. The USAF enhanced the bird's inherent ugliness by specifying a brown, green, and grey camouflage color pattern.

For fledgling F-4 airmen, initial type conversion was conducted in simulators at Davis-Monthan, DM, AFB in Tucson, Arizona. The F-4 simulators were more like procedural trainers bolted firmly to the floor. Now, flight simulators have visual simulations of the world and realistic inputs, some with motion applied to the cockpit mockup. Simulators today do everything a real airplane does, except fly, and crash. As a back-seater, I learned to operate the aircraft's fire control radar. My previous experience with radar was limited to being illuminated by those wielded by the Tennessee Highway Patrol.

Our instructors were USAF navigators, whose expertise was learned in the F-101 VooDoo interceptor's back seat. They were masters at running intercepts of bombers flying straight and level. We learned to do the same in the simulator. Later F-4 radars were modified and the back-seater training upgraded to incorporate the lessons learned from air combat over North Vietnam where the North Vietnamese fielded no bombers.

The ex-F-101 "Scope Dopes" had been infused with proper fighter pilot attitudes. They didn't fit in with the buttoned-down, conservative atmosphere at DM, a Strategic Air Command, SAC, base at the time. The local SAC Wing Commander was particularly unhappy with these uncouth fighter types, including us students, taking over the Officer's Club bar at Friday night Happy Hour.

A few wilder Scope Dopes obtained some chicken feet from the base Commissary and a black-ink rubber stamping pad. They let themselves into the WC's office very late on a Sunday night. Using the ink pad and the dead chicken feet, they stamped chicken prints all over the office. The rug, the walls, the chairs, the desk, everything got the chicken treatment. It was a statement of what they thought of the "chickenshit" WC.

Monday morning, the WC's admin assistant discovered the sacrilege and called the Security Police to come and investigate the rampant vandalism. The police examined the desk and found several classified documents, including one Secret text, all stamped with chicken feet. Classified documents are supposed to be never left unattended and Secret docs must be secured in a locked safe when not in use. Instead of nailing the perps who defiled his office, the WC received a serious security violation citation effectively ending his career. All done without a pie in the face.

When my orders came through assigning me to George AFB for F-4 flight training, I was pleased. Growing up in the South, I was the first member of my immediate family to journey across the Mississippi River for any distance. Crossing Mississippi River bridges in New Orleans didn't count, What I knew of California I learned from Annette and Tommy movies like *Beach Blanket Bingo* and the *Endless Summer* surfer movie. That last film was a Golden State impression with a sound track by the Beach Boys. Someone told me George AFB was out in the far reaches of the California desert. California has deserts? Who knew? The Beach Boys never wrote a rock and roll song about deserts. That would be The Eagles tune, Hotel California.

George AFB was in Victorville, California, in the high desert above Los Angeles. It made Big Spring look like New York City. At least you could drive down to LA in an hour or so. An hour from Big Spring put you in Abilene, Texas.

Our class learning to fly the F-4 was comprised of two groups; front seaters and back seaters. A back seater was called a GIB, Guy In Back. The front seaters were officially the AC, the Aircraft Commander, as designated in all multi-crewed USAF airplanes, although the only guy my AC commanded was me. My AC was Captain Ken Hackett an ex-GIB himself. He served one combat tour at Can Ranh Bay, South Vietnam and was upgrading to the front seat. Ken had seen the bright lights and he had heard the loud noises. He knew what he was doing and taught me a lot about how to be an effective GIB including when to shut up. Other ACs came from various backgrounds: ex T-38 IPs with a zillion hours flying time in ATC, former ADC interceptor jocks, and officers coming off staff tours.

One guy, a senior Captain, was a mystery. He flew F-86s in Korea and shot down four enemy MiG fighters. After peace broke out, he bummed around in the Air National Guard for a few years then left the service. When the Vietnam war erupted, the USAF found itself short of fighter pilots. He came back on active duty with one goal, to shoot down another MiG and be anointed an ace with the required five kills. This near-ace was an unimposing chap, short, thin, mousey looking, with little apparent military bearing. But boy could he fly! Due to his lowly rank, he often flew as #4 in a formation of four aircraft. Normally, #4 uses more fuel than the others to keep up with the formation's maneuvers. When a flight lead called for a fuel check, he always had the most fuel left. I guess flying and fighting in MiG Alley over North Korea, far from home base, will teach you that skill. After checking out in the F-4, he was assigned to Da Nang AFB in South Vietnam

The cards were stacked against him. The USAF personnel management system looked at his fitness reports and lack of Professional Military Education, PME, and decided he wasn't promotion material regardless of his expertise in the air. A Reduction In Force, RIF, program was then in effect, to reduce the number of pilots the USAF still didn't have enough of. Ten months into his combat tour, his Wing Commander had to inform him he was being culled, separated from the USAF, and returned involuntarily to civilian life. The Colonel, whose hands were tied in the matter, told the guy he was being RIF'd but not until the end of his combat tour. The WC offered him a desk job at Wing HQ or the assignment of running the Officer's Club for the next two months. He could even go on terminal leave in-country.

The Colonel said, "I'm not going to ask you to fly combat missions when the Air Force is kicking you out."

Our hero replied, "The only reason I'm here at all is to fly combat. No thanks to the kind offers."

He flew his last combat mission on the day before he rotated back to the US to become a civilian again. He never got that fifth MiG.

CHAPTER FIVE
GEORGE AFB, CA, 1967-1968

Duty in the Desert

When the intrepid aviators and junior fighter pilots of our class reported to George AFB outside Victorville, CA, we encountered a mocking tableau erected in front of Wing Headquarters. Mounted on a long plank were two toilette bowls and tanks with tandem seating. The ceramic thrones were spaced 42 inches apart, the exact distance between the front and rear seats in the F-4 . Who would do such a thing?

The F-4 training wing replaced an F-104 wing at George AFB when the Starfighters deployed to Da Nang AB in South Vietnam. The F-104s were manned by pilots who took great pride in flying all by themselves, in being single-seat, single-engine fighter jocks. Their reasoning was as the F-4 contained two crewmembers, the AC and GIB, who flew together separated by 42 inches, then those guys must hit the latrine in the same formation. They left the tandem toilet display visible as a comment on our lack of individuality and possibly our maturity.

The F-104s were a stopgap measure in Southeast Asia, used to escort B-52 bomber missions over North Vietnam. They were tasked as air superiority fighters instead of the point defense interceptors the aircraft were designed to be. They went into North Vietnam with the bombers but without any RHAW (Radar Homing And Warning) gear. They had no idea when the Bad Guys' radars were illuminating and targeting them. They also had no long-range search and track radars of their own and no beyond-visual-range missiles. Electronically naked, all they had to defend the bombers was their M61 gun and two short-range AIM-9 Sidewinder heat-seeking missiles. They also had little fuel and needed a different tanker to refuel from than other USAF fighters. The Starfighter used the probe-and-drogue system like the US Navy.

Their pilots did have one thing to protect the bombers from MiG attack; their own pink bodies. Therein lies a tale, one that infuriates me to this day.

Since WWI and the dawn of military aviation, bomber pilots have clamored for fighter escort, but their idea of an escort is someone they can see flying nearby or alongside, pacing the bomber formation. The Red Tails, the P-51 wing of WWII with all Black pilots, was famous for never leaving the bombers whom they escorted. The bomber guys loved that. Unfortunately, so did the Germans.

That is the wrong tactic to employ fighters who are escorting a bomber stream. Fighter pilots live and die on speed. "Speed is Life" is a truism in the world of fighter aviation. Kinetic energy is essential to maneuver, to chase the Bad Guys, and to intercept the enemy BEFORE they reach the bombers. It's easier to dogfight the wolves before they get into the herd.

This insecure, "stay with us" mindset has been long-ingrained in the bomber community. During the Vietnam War, the B-52s were controlled and managed by SAC HQ, whose fearless combat planners were ensconced in their impregnable redoubt outside Omaha, Nebraska. They ordained that the F-104s would stick with the B-52s and not range out in front nor off to the sides of the formation. They further decreed the last bomber, usually in a cell of three flying in trail about one half-mile apart, would have an escort at seven o'clock off its tail and another at five o'clock, keeping pace with the trio of bombers. A fully-loaded B-52 flies at about 280 Knots Indicated Air Speed, KIAS, about 320 mph. An F-104 with two external fuel tanks, two missiles and a fully-loaded gun barely flies at 280 KIAS.

The more cynical among us long believed the F-104s were not there to shoot down MiGs attacking the bombers but to soak up missiles fired at the bombers by those MiGs. That's exactly what happened in at least one instance.

My squadron commander's wife fixed me up with a nice woman on base, her next-door neighbor. She had lost her husband, an F-104 pilot. He was then listed as MIA, Missing In Action. The unlucky pilot was stooging along at 280 knots in trail with a cell of three B-52s when an unseen MiG-21 fired a heat-seeking missile up the Starfighter's tailpipe. The resulting explosion ripped the Starfighter apart. His wingman tried to turn on and attack the MiG, but by the time he accelerated enough to manage a tight turn, the MiG was long-gone. The wingman spotted a good parachute in the air but no signal came from any emergency radio and the doomed pilot's name never appeared on any Prisoner Of War, POW, list.

Some SAC general, safe behind his mahogany desk in Omaha, probably felt this was a righteous trade-off. He, and we, lost one lowly fighter pilot and one soon-to-be obsolete aircraft instead of a work-horse B-52 with its six-man crew. I would have loved to see this desk jockey explain that terrible bargain to a certain distraught widow in Victorville, CA.

The maybe-widow would have liked a deeper, more personal, relationship with me, but I just couldn't do it. I kept remembering her husband may have still been alive in some hell-hole prison camp. She needed emotional support more than sex.

Somehow, it never dawned on the SAC brain trust to unleash the F-104s to take down the MiGs before they got to the bombers. This pig-headed approach to air combat in 1972 cost the United States of America at least a dozen B-52s over Hanoi during Operation Linebacker II. A SAC planner, a one-star general, in Nebraska, dictated B-52 bomber tactics identical to those used in WWII, a steady stream of giant bombers following one another in a predictable flight path. The big birds were lined up like tin ducks in a shooting gallery for the Vietnamese Surface-to-Air Missiles, SAMs. To make matters even worse, this numbskull ordered the bombers to execute a post-target-max-rate-turn after dropping their bombs. This turn was designed for the delivery of nuclear weapons, not iron bombs. The 45-degree banked turn, over Hanoi, negated the bombers self-defense electronic countermeasures, i.e., jamming, and exposed the poor bastards flying them to the Bad Guys' radars and SAMs. I wonder if the general was proud of what he did.

As a result of this criminal misuse and due to the Starfighter's poor reliability (the jet was rushed into production one or two years early, before the glitches had been worked out) the hapless F-104s suffered a 30% loss rate during their brief deployment to Da Nang and later to Udorn, Thailand. Knowing this early-in the-war history, we left the dual toilet display up in front of Wing HQ. It seemed like the right thing to do while we trained to replace the F-104s symbolically if not actually.

During the Vietnam war, a combat tour for a fighter pilot was exactly one year or 100 missions over North Vietnam, whichever came first. Years later, I met an ex-F-104 pilot who logged the requisite 100 combat mission over the North. This feat, in the face of that 30% loss rate, earned him an early return and the Big Brass Balls honorary award. But we flew the Phantom, not the Starfighter.

The F-4 Phantom was a formidable machine; solid, heavy, a serious aircraft. All the other planes I had previously flown, light planes and jet trainers, seemed toy-like in comparison. Those early birds were built lightly, with thin aluminum sheeting, stamped wing ribs, and lots of plastics. Even the supersonic T-38 seemed inconsequential compared to the mighty F-4. The fighter jet seemed to be machined out of a solid piece of aluminum or maybe steel. The Phantom carried more internal fuel than the T-38's gross weight. Those two J-79 engine intakes were the size of manholes. The cockpits were also huge with two rows of panels on each consol. When I eventually got into the front cockpit, I found I could put my legs up and stretch out. It even had a bullet (and-bird) proof windscreen for attacking bombers equipped with tail gunners.

In contrast to the White Rocket, landing the Phantom was a piece of cake. With the T-38, the trick was to roll it gently on the runway. During testing, the F-4 was dropped vertically from 10 feet and nothing broke. In the Phantom, a landing required no finesse, you just plunked it down and put out the drag chute. It was equally easy to take-off. You just pulled the control stick full aft, lit the afterburners, released the wheel brakes and held the stick against the ejection seat until the nose was ten degrees above the horizon.

For all its heft, over 30,000 pounds empty, those thunderous J-79's would accelerate the bird like a rocket sled. In level flight, all aircraft generate drag when producing lift. This is called induced drag. For max acceleration in the F-4, we would push over until we floated up from the seats weightless at zero G. With no induced drag and in afterburner, the jet would push you in the back. Nowadays, jet fighters have even higher thrust-to-weight ratios. But back then, the Phantom was the top performing jet fighter in the world and I got to fly it. However, my training at George AFB was more than just airborne maneuvers.

The Replacement Training Unit, the RTU, squadron was manned by fighter pilots, one and all. The Commander, Lt/Col Dan Farr, had been featured in a book by Elaine Shepard, a war correspondent. I read *The Doom Pussy*, a breathless chronicle about flying B-57 Canberra tactical bombers out of Da Nang. "DOOM" stood for the Da Nang Officers Open Mess, the Officers Club. The rest of the title refers to an imaginary, one-eyed, black cat, not what you think, so get your mind out of the gutter right now. Some of the guys in the wing had been on the famous

Operation Bolo mission with legendary Wing Commander and fighter pilot, Col Robin Olds, when they shot down seven North Vietnamese MiG-21s. This score eliminated the Bad Guys' entire inventory of MiG-21 fighters, giving rise to the concern that we shot up all the breeding stock. However, the Russians replaced the losses straightaway.

These guys not only instructed us in how to fly fighters, they taught us how to be fighter pilots. There are pilots who can fly fighter planes who are not fighter pilots. Test pilots come to mind. The key is a mindset, a way of looking at life and sometimes at death. It's about how you approach your mission, about outwardly not taking yourself too seriously while taking great pride internally in what you can do with an airplane. It's about standing and delivering, meaning what you say, and saying what you mean. How is this different from any other military ethos? It just is. Author Richard S. Bach in his classic aviation/adventure book, *Stranger to the Ground*, said it far better than I can and believe me, I've tried to in my books.

After getting the ACs through transition, learning how to take off, fly formation, and land safely, the next item on the syllabus was air combat conducted in two phases; Basic Fighter Maneuvers, BFM, and Air Combat Maneuvers, ACM. The training was rudimentary. We were taught and we practiced the maneuvers, formations, and tactics perfected in the Korean War of the early 1950s. Some common drills were; the low-speed yo-yo, the high-speed yo-yo, and the rolling scissors. All of these were aimed at getting a fighter in position for a kill using guns, which we didn't have any of. In Korea, the USAF F-86 Sabrejets and their adversaries, the MiG-15s, were sub-sonic, low-wing-loaded, underpowered aircraft which had trouble gaining altitude and in using the vertical dimension. These early single-seat fighters turned tightly, but lost energy rapidly when doing so. They also handled well at low airspeed and high AOA. Phantoms did none of this.

The F-4 was a high-wing-loaded, supersonic jet with two crewmembers. It climbed like a homesick angel and thrived at high speed. At low speed and high-AOA, it handled like a hog on roller skates. Its forté was the high-speed, missile engagement arena. Did I mention we didn't have a gun for close combat?

Why the archaic tactics? In Korea, the F-86s feasted on the MiGs, killing the inept North Korean and sometimes Chinese pilots like in a turkey shoot. Occasionally, our guys would encounter a visiting Russian veteran of WWII who knew his stuff, but not often. After the war and with the emphasis on a 'strategic" Air Force in the 1950's, air combat tactics were not updated. That was perceived to be not needed as evidenced by the notional 17-1 kill ratio (the actual ratio was about half that), so why spend the brain power and jet fuel to come up with tactics which actually fit the aircraft we flew and the missiles we deployed at the time of the unpleasantness in Vietnam?

It was great fun though, watching my AC throw the relatively huge Phantom around like it was an F-86. Air-to-air combat is the ultimate thrill ride, an e-coupon, a main-lined adrenalin fix. Six Gs, followed instantly by zero Gs with the sky and the ground trading places in the canopy overhead in a matter of seconds. My job as the GIB was to keep my eyes peeled for other aircraft and to stay awake when I weighed effectively 1000 pounds under 6 Gs and when I could barely keep my head up. Practicing air combat is the most fun you can have with your clothes on.

In the Vietnam air war, our Korean-era tactics and formations worked, sort of, at first against the inexperienced and outnumbered North Vietnamese. As the war dragged on and on and on and with Russian help, the Bad Guys worked out tactics to defeat us. Our kill ratio went from five-to-one to even money. We had to change and we did. We even got a gun.

As the GIB, my duties also involved navigation, a skill at which I was mediocre at best. A relaxed portion of the flying syllabus was leaning how to aerial re-fuel. This involved putting the jet in close under the tail of a KC-135 tanker which filled the canopy above us. Then the boom operator stuck a stiff extension boom into an open receptacle on the F-4. Insert the sexual analogy of your choice HERE. My AC, an ex-GIB, was an old hand at aerial refueling having learned the skill from the back seat. So, on a refueling mission with a flight of four, we could relax and fly formation off the tanker's wing. From that perch we could observe the ex-ATC and ex-ADC jocks clumsy, fumbling attempts to get hooked up. It was like watching a high-school house party. During my first combat tour, I too learned how to refuel while operating from the back seat. It was the most difficult skill I ever tried to perfect.

Our practice refueling area was a long race-track shaped pattern over the high Sierras, running north and south along and over the rocky peaks reaching for the sky. We were at 22,000 feet. The first mission was on a blue-bright morning in February. A winter storm had blown through during the night covering the mountain range with a new, pristine blanket of snow. As is common after a cold front passes, the air was gin-clear with visibility as far as the eye can see. The view was spectacular, snow-covered, jagged peaks beneath us, the flat brown desert to our east and off in the far west, the blue Pacific Ocean. This was the sort of view non-aviators seldom get to enjoy.

On our first lap around the track, I looked ahead of the formation and saw a sight which I can picture to this day. I spotted a large, alpine lake of the darkest indigo blue in a bowl ringed with pure white snowy mountains. The lake was slightly oblong, oriented north and south. It was matched nowhere else for size or beauty in the Sierras passing slowly beneath us. I spoke up on the cockpit intercom.

"Wow! That's really pretty, that lake. Do you know it is? I'm the navigator, I have a right to know."

The answer came back, dripping with sarcasm, "That's Lake Tahoe."

He didn't have to add, "you moron," the taunt was implied but still unmistakable. Later I found out Lake Tahoe is on the state line, half of it is in California and half in Nevada although that fact isn't apparent from the air. Another winter, I drove up to Tahoe for a long weekend. It was, and is, one of the world's most spectacular scenes. Despite me never having heard of it, Lake Tahoe was one of the few places in the world where, when I first saw it up close, I asked myself, "What can I do to earn a living so I can live here?" I never found an answer.

CHAPTER SIX
GEORGE AFB, CA

Diving at Planet Earth

One skill set we weren't taught in UPT was dive bombing. This ordnance delivery technique was perfected and popularized by the German Air Force, the Luftwaffe, in WWII. Other air arms used the technique but not as well as the Germans. Their Ju 87 "Stuka" dive bombers could take out individual tanks, usually Russian or Polish, with small bombs dropped individually. While exhibiting perfect marksmanship, this activity wasn't popular with the Russians or the Poles or the French.

Level bombing, as practiced early in tactical aviation and by large aircraft today, has a major drawback. When a bomb falls away from a bomber flying straight and level, it is traveling across the ground at the same speed as the bomber and continues to do so. The bomb's forward throw, its flight path, projects far ahead of the release point. A slight error in heading, a fraction of a degree, puts the bomb off target to the left or right. A tiny error in release timing puts the bomb way in front of or way past the target, i.e., long or short. Dive bombing, hurling the bomb at the target from a steep dive, reduces the effects of these sources of misses. Also, with a greatly reduced time of flight, the bomb is less affected by the mischief induced by wayward winds. The only negative to dive bombing is that to hurl the bomb at the target, the delivery aircraft, including me, must to dive at the target as well.

Dive bombing is accomplished as follows: The gunsight is depressed below the fighter's flight path at a pre-calculated angle. If the gunsight is on the target and the flight parameters are met, the bomb will hit in the general vicinity of the target. This requires the F-4 pilot to achieve those parameters with precision. They are; dive angle, usually 45 degrees; airspeed, usually 450 KIAS, (about 520 mph): and release altitude, for training usually 4500 feet. Getting the gunsight on the target takes practice, achieving the right dive angle comes with experience, and the aircraft seems to want to fly at 450 knots in a 45-degree dive. The critical parameter is release altitude, too high and the bomb drops short. To low and the bomb sails long. Compounding the problem is the fact that at 450 knots in a 45-degree dive, the altimeter unwinds very quickly and the AC doesn't have enough bandwidth to monitor it closely. That's where I, the GIB, came in as the World's First Talking Altimeter.

My job during dive bomb practice was to call out the altitude and then call "Pickle" to announce it was time to drop the bomb and let's please start pulling out of this dive right now.

Why "Pickle?" In WWII, in large multi-engined bombers such as the B-17, B-24, and B-26, the bombardier held in his hand a bomb release handle on the end of an electrical cord. The item was the size, shape, and color of a large cucumber dill pickle. On the end of the "pickle" was a red button which, when pushed, electrically released the bombs. Naturally, the red tit was known as the "pickle button." It soon followed that all bomb release buttons, even the one on fighter control stick grips, were knows as "pickle buttons." Hence, "Push the pickle button" became just "Pickle."

Not that we dropped real bombs. Training was conducted with five-pound practice bombs, painted blue, about the size of a bowling pin with fins on the back. These units contained a small explosive charge which emitted a puff of white smoke on impact. This marker allowed scoring of the bomb's distance from the intended target.

Bomb accuracy is measured by charting a large number of impacts and drawing a circle with the target at its center. The circle's perimeter includes one half of the impact points with the other half lying outside the circle. The circle's diameter is the Circular Error Probable or CEP. Our goal in training was to score a CEP of 120 feet, meaning half of our five-pound bombs hit withing 120 feet of the target with the rest further out. If this doesn't sound like precision bombing that's because it wasn't.

This inherent inaccuracy in manual dive bombing gave rise to smart bombs mid-way through the South East Asia war once the technology matured. Smart bombs know where the target is while dumb bombs know only where the ground is. So, we practiced with our tiny, dumb bombs. It wasn't until my first combat mission that I saw real, live ordnance delivered. I witnessed a circular Mach One shock wave, made visible by high atmospheric humidity, radiate out across a North Vietnamese rice paddy from a 2000-pound dumb bomb. The sight was spectacular.

But how did Luftwaffe pilots plink single tanks with small bombs? The Germans reduced all the error-producing parts of the geometry to zero by diving at 90 degrees. I'm glad we didn't do that. In a vertical dive, release altitude is not important, which was workable as the GIB in a Stuka rode facing backwards with no altimeter. His armed with a 30-caliber machine gun, his job was to defend the Stuka from attacking Royal Air Force, RAF, Spitfires or Hurricanes. This usually didn't work leading to RAF "Stuka Shoots."

In WWII, the straight and level CEPs racked up by the large, four-engined bombers was about a quarter-mile. Half the bombs hit within a quarter mile of the target, half elsewhere. This was acceptable when bombing something like the city of Berlin but useless for tactical targets unless many bombs were dropped which was the usual case.

Another phase of training concerned nuclear weapons delivery. We didn't expect to rain nukes down on North Vietnam, but other F-4 units around the world did have a nuclear mission. We needed to prepare for any follow-on assignment once we finished with SEA or it was finished with us. The trick in nuke weapons delivery isn't achieving pin-point accuracy. Exact placement doesn't matter before a multi-megaton fireball explosion blossoms. The challenge was to Exit Stage Right, or Left, before the blast. Now we have nukes with terminal guidance which can hit within a few feet of Ground Zero. Why bother? Consider the possible targets, not whole cities, but something like the entrance tunnel to an underground uranium enrichment facility in Iran. It's sort of like bombing the Death Star's ventilation shaft in "Star Wars."

One night, at the Officers Club bar, after a few adult beverages, maybe a few too many, a bunch us of budding F-4 pilots were discussing the nuclear mission. The obvious question which everyone wanted to ask but few wanted to answer was, "If called upon to do so, would you drop a nuke, say on North Korea, and kill maybe a million people?" A major, late of ADC, responded, "I'd consider it an honor." For some reason, that answer gave me cold chills.

Later that night while I stared at the ceiling of my palatial suite in the BOQ, trying to keep the room from spinning, I asked myself the same question. I came to the conclusion that since I swore an oath to execute all legal orders, I would indeed drop a nuke. That is if the order didn't come from some Strangelovian character like Brigadier General Jack D. Ripper, the fictional SAC Wing Commander. In any case, I would not consider it an honor.

George AFB wasn't all flying and training. One December night, I proved you can get four adults, two guys with two gals, in a Corvette convertible with the top up. I then proceeded to prove you can spin a Corvette 360 degrees on a snow-covered I-15 and not put a scratch on the car nor a bruise on anyone. I learned a valuable lesson from this episode. No matter what dumb-assed stunt I pulled, things would always work out in the end. Right.

We finished our F-4 check-out with no losses, nobody washed out, and nobody got killed. Our orders came through. I was assigned to the 8th Tactical Fighter Wing, the "Wolfpack," at Ubon Royal Thai AFB, Ubon Ratchathani, Thailand. I was stoked. The Wolfpack was Cols Robin Old's and Chappy James's old outfit. The wing was famous for taking the fight deep into North Vietnam. Chappy James was one of the original Tuskegee airmen, a Black pilot. Naturally the pair were known as Blackman and Robin. Also, I got to live in Thailand which was way better than South Vietnam. But first, survival training, the real kind, not in the Great Dismal Swamp, reared its ugly head.

At the Fairchild AFB, Washington survival school I learned when I didn't eat, I got hungry and when I didn't sleep, I got tired. I guess some of the survival training could have been useful particularly the mock Prisoner Of War, camp. The very motivated instructors taught us the techniques we could expect the Bad Guys to use on us to try and break our will to resist while in captivity. By this time, we had a few hundred POWs in the "Hanoi Hilton." None had been returned so we had no idea how they were being treated or tortured. The training was based on experiences in Korea. Later, my roommate at Ubon, Bill Schwertfeger, spent three years as a POW. After the SEA war, our POW training was upgraded to include the new and novel ways of communist captors.

Sea Survival training at Homestead AFB, outside of Miami, FL was way different, fun even, like a week-long swim party but with no bikini-clad girls. I had been a competitive swimmer in high school and had passed the Georgia Tech "Drownproofing" course so the water activities were easy. Some of the less aquatic guys had to tough it out. The USAF, saving air fare, flew us to Florida in a C-130 "Hercules" four-turbo-prop transport. Somehow, two loading manifests got mixed up and we were sent out on a "Herky-Bird" which was already full of cargo. We flew south draped all over various crates and bits of machinery.

Graduation exercise at Homestead was a full-dress rehearsal for a sea survival situation. I donned a parachute and was towed aloft by a USAF rescue boat and yes, there are USAF boats. Several hundred feet in the air, I dropped the tow rope and floated down to a water landing. In college, I was a sky diver so the parachute drill was old hat. The trick is to not get tangled in the chute or shroud lines in the water and to not get towed across Biscayne Bay by a wind-filled chute. Ditching the chute, I then climbed into my one-person life raft and bailed it out. For the rest of the exercise, I was supposed to deploy all my signaling devices and practice using them to signal to a simulated rescue helicopter. However, a bunch of us had closed down a bar in Fort Lauderdale the previous night. I was hung-over, big time. I went to sleep in the raft rocking with the gentle swells. The other guys knew this and were picked up by the rescue boat. I woke up to find an empty sea, no boat, no helo, just merciless sun, and water. I thought my survival drill was turning into the real thing until the boat came back for me. I strongly suspect my esteemed fellow classmates put the instructors up to this.

The final test for my survival merit badge was Jungle Survival at Clark AFB, in the Philippines. That too was great fun. I filled a bucket list item by cutting a jungle vine and swinging across a ravine like Tarzan. What they don't show you in the Tarzan movies is what happens when you get to the other side, impact with the tree.

CHAPTER SEVEN
UBON RATCHATHANI, THAILAND.
1968-1969

The Older I Get, the Better I Was

I served two tours in "C" Flight, 433rd Tactical Fighter Squadron, "Satan's Angels," 8th Tactical Fighter Wing, "The Wolfpack," at Ubon Ratchathani Royal Thai Air Force Base in the flat plains and rice paddies of northeastern Thailand. During these two, year-long tours, I flew 375 combat missions over North Vietnam, Laos, and Cambodia. Our wing was out-country dedicated specializing in high-threat targets and night interdiction along the Ho Chi Minh trail. I never dropped ordinance in South Viet Nam. With our one-pass-and-haul-ass tactics, our bombing accuracy, or lack thereof, prevented us from working troops-in-contact, never in close proximity to friendly forces. Or else they might not have stayed friendly. Later, when we introduced laser-guided bombs to the Bad Guys, the equation changed. Then, it was one bomb, one target and what's next on today's target list.

All these adventures have been chronicled in my book, *War for the Hell of It: A Fighter Pilot's View of Vietnam*. I won't repeat myself.

CHAPTER EIGHT
MACDILL AFB, TAMPA, FL, 1969

Upgrade by the Bay

After one combat tour at Ubon, Thailand, I returned stateside to upgrade to Aircraft Commander in the F-4. To get this assignment, I was required by the USAF to volunteer for a second combat tour, which I was happy to sign up for. All my life, I wanted to fly fighters in combat with the USAF. A saying making the rounds then held true, "It's a crummy war, but it's the only one we have."

This dynamic illustrates one of the major mistakes I think the USA made in Vietnam. Whether in the air with 100 missions over North Vietnam, or for one year, whichever came first, or on the ground with a one-year tour (13 months for the US Marines), we combatants could see the end of our service on the day we arrived in-country. All we had to do was survive that period, regardless of whether the war was being won or not. In other conflicts, WWI, WWI, Korea, GIs were sent out for the duration of the war. This gave them a powerful incentive to finish the job and then go home. A key point is, if the GIs felt the war wasn't being conducted to win, they would have complained mightily. Letters home, letters to the newspapers, reports to their representatives in Congress, interviews with the press, the pressure would have been there. No one wants to fight indefinitely in an unwinnable war. In the later stages of the Vietnam war, we saw a rapid erosion of morale and a loss of the will to fight. Officers were "fragged" with hand grenades in their tents. Guys shot themselves in the foot to get sent home wounded. Combat operations were conducted half-heartedly if at all. Late in the war, when I was training F-4 replacement pilots, my students refused to practice 45-degree dive bombing. They felt steep dives were too hazardous for too little gain. In a way they were right. We should have fought to win and left our folks there until the job done or it was obvious it couldn't be done, which was more likely. Complicating matters is our national can-do attitude. We as a nation are used to winning wars. We find it very hard to admit to a lost cause. When it became apparent that the South Vietnamese were an unreliable ally, we should have had them shape up or we should have gone home. Sadly, this approach is a mistake, in my view, we keep making as a country. We sign up for unwinnable wars, Iraq and Afghanistan come to mind, and then we let the troops cycle in and out, never finishing the job nor folding a losing hand.

Regardless of the dismal geo-political aspects of the war at the time, I jumped on the F-4 upgrade program like a duck on a June bug. I already knew how to operate the aircraft; take-off, fly formation, aerial refuel, and land, all from the back seat. Now I had to learn was how to do it from the front cockpit. This did not come without effort. On my first transition flight, I set up for my first landing as an AC. Landing from the back seat required I look left, around the front ejection seat, and to conduct the landing looking out of the left front-quarter windscreen. As I lined up on final, the IP in the rear cockpit said, "Ed what the hell are you doing? Sit up straight!" I was leaning far left. I sat up straight, as ordered, and VOILA! there was the runway dead ahead in the windscreen. The now unobstructed view made landing the jet much easier.

Most USAF fighter base runways measure 150 feet wide, occasionally 200 feet. MacDill AFB had been a SAC base with giant bombers stationed there. The runway was 500 feet across. If, when landing, you relied on the same sight picture out the sides of the windscreen to touch down, the aircraft would stall 100 feet in the air making for a very solid impact. This took some getting used to. What didn't take getting used to was Tampa, Florida.

Compared to Big Spring and Victorville, Tampa was paradise. Good restaurants of various ethnic backgrounds (I loved the Cuban food), sandy beaches the color of refined sugar, lively night life, good bars, and a multitude of interesting women. Those attributes are not listed in order of desirability.

Tampa was not all beers and skittles, whatever that means. MacDill AFB juts into Tampa Bay. An ejection on takeoff or landing involves a swim. Then, the bay was so polluted if you did take a dip, it meant 48 hours in the base hospital to cleanse your system of any toxins you might have ingested or adsorbed. I understand it is much cleaner now. Once I was airborne, I forgot about the possibility of swimming in raw sewage.

Learning air combat from the front seat was a hoot, but the process took some adjustments to my skill set. In the T-38, as I recounted earlier in this book, you could fly a White Rocket mission with your flying boots planted flat on the cockpit floor. Not so in the F-4. At high AOA and low airspeed, the Phantom exhibited severe adverse yaw. What's that? The aerodynamics are technical and beyond the scope of this book. What it means is when you roll the aircraft to the right with the stick the nose slices left. Or vice-versa. In most aircraft, the name for this phenomenon is "Spin Entry." You could catch it, center the stick, and fly out of the incipient spin if you acted quickly enough. But if you were looking back over your shoulder, or having a bad day, you could easily spin the jet.

A spin in the F-4 was not steady-state and relatively comfortable as in the Tweety-Bird or Jet Provost. The Phantom's nose oscillated up and down by 30-45 degrees. The wings rocked plus or minus 45 degrees. The rate of rotation of the nose would speed up and slow down during each turn of the spin. Not a fun E-Coupon ride. It seemed to us that the "Golden Arm" test pilots of the Edwards AFB Flight Test Center and of McDonnel Aircraft would change the recommended spin recovery procedures on a yearly basis. When in a spin, if you couldn't remember that year's technique there was one action which always worked. Put out the drag chute. The drag chute was used to slow the aircraft down on the runway after landing, saving the wheel brakes. In a spin, the chute would snap the nose down, breaking the rotation. For a few seconds, the massive F-4 would be hanging vertically from the drag chute like the world's largest and ugliest Christmas tree ornament. Then the airspeed would rapidly climb from zero and the chute would tear away in the wind stream. Back at the base, you had to explain to the maintenance troops why they needed to spring for a new drag chute. The operations people, the Squadron Commander, or the Operations Officer, would never criticize the use of the chute to recover from a spin. Better to lose a chute than an aircraft.

There was one control technique which always worked to prevent spin entry. At high AOA, you had to avoid the use of any aileron at all. By keeping the stick centered and rolling the aircraft with the rudder pedals spins seldom reared their twirly heads. That took some practice to learn. In the 1970's the Phantom was retro-fitted with slats on the wings' leading edges. These smoothed the air flow at high AOA and virtually eliminated adverse yaw. On a slatted F-4 you could actually roll the aircraft with the stick at slow airspeed and high AOA, just like a normal airplane. Why this modification wasn't included in 1950s when the aircraft was first built is beyond me.

At George AFB, our air combat practice arena was, and I'm not making this up, over Death Valley, CA. At MacDill, we practiced air fighting above the Gulf of Mexico. Over Death Valley, with high mountains on each side and a flat desert below, it was easy to judge your altitude, or lack thereof, by looking outside. Not so over the Gulf. Water displays what is called a "fractal" surface. It looks the same no matter how far from it you are. This phenomenon is best explained without an airplane in the picture. In parachuting into the sea, you want to release your chute before it settles down, tangling over you in the water or starts dragging you across the ocean like fishing lure for sharks. The trick is to pull the harness release tabs just as your boots hit the drink. Otherwise, you might drop 100 feet. It is that hard to judge height over water. In air combat the problem is the same only it happens much quicker. Fortunately, by this time, I acquired my own talking altimeter, my GIB, to keep us from flying out of the sky and into the ocean.

Another challenge of air combat training at the time was we only fought against each other, in F-4s. I learned what to do and what not to do when in a dogfight with a Phantom. As noted, ad nauseum, the F-4 has a certain set of unique flight characteristics. By and large these attributes are the opposite of those exhibited by our likely adversaries, Soviet Union-produced MiGs. If we had gone to war with an air arm flying Phantoms, such as the US Navy or the Royal Air Force, I would have known how to win. Against MiGs, not so much.

The authorities at the time stated air combat training with dissimilar aircraft was unsafe. I felt air combat with an aircraft such as a MiG-21, which I had never seen, would be unsafe. In the 1970s when the kill ratio over the North Vietnamese MiGs approached one-to-one, we wised up and began training with other types of jets. We even acquired and flew our own squadron of MiGs as mock adversaries. More on this later. Read on.

I did get in some unofficial dissimilar air combat maneuvering though. Across Tampa Bay in St. Petersburg, the Cavalier Aircraft Company rebuilt P-51 propeller-driven Mustangs fighters from WWII. They took war surplus aircraft and converted them into expensive toys for rich people to fly. Once, I was on the downwind leg of an instrument landing pattern, but in clear air. I needed the practice. My GIB was doing his duty keeping a lookout for airborne traffic while I focused on the gauges, called out, "We have a bogy at our right five o'clock, one mile, slightly high, inbound."

I whirled around in the ejection seat and looked behind us. We were being "bounced" by a P-51! While we were at 200 knots, he was moving at the speed of high-octane aviation gas. This would not do. I slammed the landing gear up, retracted the flaps, plugged in the afterburners, cancelled our instrument flight plan, and turned to meet the threat coming from a war long ago. Check that. I tried to turn into the attack. The next thing I saw was a P-51 at our six o'clock pulling lead for a simulated gun kill. My GIB and I were meat on the table. Score one for the US Army Air Corps. I rolled out level, cancelled the afterburners, and rocked my wings, the universal signal for "I give up. You win." I then watched as the Mustang departed toward St. Pete, his snarling Merlin V-12 engine twirling a big four-bladed propeller. The pilot was probably rehearsing his story of aerial victory for the bar crowd that night. That was the closest I came to dissimilar air combat, but not with a MiG.

However, not all of us at MacDill were unfamiliar with MiGs. One of our IPs was scheduled to attend a tactics conference down at Homestead AFB, about 50 miles south of Miami. He and one of the student GIBs flew an F-4 down. At that time, every Air Force base had several Jeeps or pick-up trucks with large signs on the back reading "Follow Me" in yellow letters. The maintenance troops would meet visiting aircraft at the end of the runway. After jettisoned the drag chute, you followed them to where they parked transient aircraft.

The IP arrived at the transient ramp and was preparing to shut down the aircraft. He and the GIB opened their canopies and waited until the ground crew chocked the wheels before killing the engines. The GIB looked up and saw a tiny, silver, swept-wing aircraft over the field. He notified the AC, "Look up. An F-86 is landing." The AC saw the little jet and yelled, "Holy shit, that's no F-86, it's a MiG-17. Cubans are attacking the base!" Homestead AFB was within easy range of MiGs out of Cuba.

In the F-4E, we flew with the M-61 gun fully loaded with practice ammunition at all times. This weight in the nose allowed us to fill a tank in the tail, giving 500 more pounds of fuel on board. To prevent a screw-up, one which might spray 20 mm slugs over South Florida, the gun had a safety pin inserted. This steel pin, about the size of a wooden lead pencil, had a red flag attached. It kept the gun from firing no matter how badly the moron in the cockpit mismanaged the armament switches. The gun and the safety pin were behind an access door in the aircraft's nose.

Intending to get airborne and gun the attacking MiG, the AC gave the ground crew hand signals to pull the chocks and arm the gun by pulling the safety pin. The signal for the gun was making a pistol with your thumb and fingers and flexing your thumb, like playing cowboys. The gun would have been armed, if at all, in the arming area at the take-off end of the runway. It was never armed on the transient ramp after a flight.

The befuddled ground crewman went to his "follow me" truck to get his headset and mike, allowing him to speak to the aircrew. Once plugged in, the AC told him, "Cubans are attacking the base! Arm the gun and pull the chocks!" Before the poor guy could open the access door and pull the safety pin, the AC said, "Never mind, We'll shut down."

Both the AC and the GIB spotted another "follow me" truck moving slowly down the ramp way. Taxiing behind the truck was a MiG-17 with Cuban Air Force markings. Both aircraft shut down, their engines slowly spinning to a stop. Dismounted, the three pilots met between the parked jets along with the ground crew. None of the Americans spoke any Spanish, which would not be the case now. The Cuban pilot took off his knee board which was top quality. USAF knee boards, used to take notes during flight, were junk, no one used them. The Cuban handed the AC his knee board, of Russian origin, a gift from Communist Cuba. This unique event occurred before airfield security became vital after 911. It took a few minutes for the Security Police to arrive and take the Cuban away. They also confiscated the knee board.

The defector, a Major in the Cuban Air Force, was granted political asylum, the MiG was returned to Cuba (!). No one knows what happened to the knee board The GIB was sent to remedial aircraft recognition training. Years later, an unprepared Homestead AFB was wiped off the map by a hurricane, with no Cuban involvement. More years later, an equally unready Tyndall AFB, FL was also trashed by a hurricane. It seems the USAF's strategy for avoiding hurricane damage is to hope they come ashore somewhere else.

I too had my moments of frustration and chagrin. One phase of our training was night ground attack. It's a toss up whether this mission is more hazardous to the Bad Guys or the aircrews, the Good Guys. Remember that 120-foot CEP for dive-bombing? You can double or triple that at night, on a good night.

The mission one night was to bomb some junked trucks parked on the Avon Park gunnery range in central Florida. An air-to-ground gunnery range is a large piece of real estate with practice targets on it along with range towers for the spotters who scored the bomb impacts. Sometimes, on the nuclear range, enormous bulls-eyes were bladed into the desert, or in this case the swamp, for self-scoring. For night missions, the scoring towers were un-manned, those guys were no fools, no telling where the bombs would land in the dark. Only the range officer was on duty to clear us on and off the range in our flight of two F-4s.

Night bombing missions in Central Florida were an exercise in weirdness. The gunnery ranges used by jets from George AFB were out in the middle of the Mojave Desert surrounded by hundreds of square miles of blackness. No one lived nearby. They call it Death Valley for a reason. Of course, the real ranges for ordnance delivery along the Ho Chi Minh trail in Laos and in North Vietnam were totally pitch-black. The night was illuminated only by the occasional fiery bomb blast or the sprinkler-lights of cluster bomblets detonating. In contrast, night strikes from MacDill AFB were like flying missions into Beverly Hills. As we left the Tampa/St. Pete area and its bright lights and climbed, we could see to the North, the glow of Orlando. To the South lay, on the other side of the Everglades, Fort Lauderdale, and Miami spread out like a carpet of light. Ahead was Daytona, a relatively dim complex by comparison. In the middle of all this manufactured light was the stretch of nothingness in the center of the state. Somewhere in the dark void was our target.

I had trouble taking this mission seriously. There were no guns trying to shoot us down, no mountains to run into, and no SAMs to avoid. Catcher and philosopher Yogi Berra once said he "nonchalanted" a fly ball in left field, dropping the baseball for an error. I was about to nonchalant the ground attack exercise.

The plan was simple, like the pilots. As fight lead, I would take a navigation fix off the rotating beacon at Avon Park AFB, then use that fix to find the unlit bombing range in the night. My GIB and I would fly over the range at 2000 feet and release a parachute flare. This was a piece of ordnance about the size, shape, and weight of a wooden fence post. After release, when the fuse timed out, the flare would ignite its load of magnesium powder while floating down under a small parachute. The magnesium would combust for two or three minutes, the heat of the fire rising and keeping the parachute inflated, slowing the descent. The intense, white light would illuminate a few football fields worth of the target area. My wingman, Number Two, would bomb the truck hopefully located under the flare's light. Then we would reverse roles and he would dispense a flare for me.

Everything went smoothly, we got a fix on the beacon and pickled off the flare. When it ignited, instead of seeing a few junk trucks under the glow, all we could see stretching out in all four quadrants was rows and rows of citrus trees fading off into the far darkness. Not a good sign. We fell back, rejoined the formation, and tried to figure out what went wrong. My GIB solved the screw-up. Military airfields have a rotating beacon on a tower which projects two white flashes and one green burst on each rotation. The beacon I chose to fly off of was showing one white flash and one green, signifying a civilian airfield. We had taken our flare run fix on Sebring Airport, a thoroughly peaceful establishment nowhere near any gunnery range.

Once we figured this out, the mission went much better although the range officer could have eaten his midnight snack sitting in the cab of a target truck with no worries about being hit by practice bombs. The next day, I fully expected to get a call from one of the Judge Advocate General office's lawyers (who were not nearly as good-looking as the characters on the JAG TV show) informing me a local orange grove had been torched by a burning parachute flare and the US Government was on the hook for damages. However, the local "Florida Boys," the farmers, were very supportive of the military and nothing ever came of the incident.

One thing I didn't screw up was getting married. The previous year, 1st Lt. Bob Scott was killed when his F-100 was lost in South Vietnam. It was his third combat mission. He left behind a foxy, very intelligent, blonde widow from Chicagoland, as the locals call it. Pat had the looks, killer legs, and the world's most adorable toddler, Carolyn, a little girl who was equally blonde. We fell in love and were married at the MacDill Officers club. Guys flew in from all over, but due to weather problems, several were delayed in route, arriving the morning of the ceremony. It was the first wedding I ever saw with guys in baggy, smelly, flight suits in attendance.

After graduation and being frocked as an AC, I was destined to deploy back to the war, leaving my new bride and daughter in Tampa. The local squadron commander drew me aside and told me that I was welcome to return to MacDill as an IP after my combat tour. They wanted me back. That complement made me feel like I was getting a handle of this business of flying fighters. But first, there was work to be done in SEA.

CHAPTER NINE
DA NANG AFB,
SOUTH VIETNAM, 1970

Dang. Da Nang

Toward the end of our class's F-4 upgrade training, our orders for SEA and for more combat came through. I got assigned to the 366th TFW, "The Gunfighters," at Da Nang AFB located in the northern part of South Vietnam. This posting was disappointing as I hoped to return to Thailand. However, the Da Nang assignment offered me the opportunity to learn some new job skills. The Phantoms from Da Nang flew close air support missions in South Vietnam as well as strike missions in Laos. At Ubon, close air support wouldn't be on the flight schedule. The 8th TFW, the "Wolfpack," was dedicated to out-country, high-threat-area missions.

The Gunfighters acquired their awesome nickname from an attempt to remedy the no-gun problem with the F-4. US Air Force Systems Command boffins installed a M-61 20 mm Vulcan cannon with a large ammunition magazine in a hollowed-out fuel tank, mounting the contraption on the Phantom's centerline external station. It wasn't an elegant solution. Serious drawbacks were obvious from the start. The pod with 1200 bullets weighed over 1700 pounds. Whether you used it or not, you still had to lug around nearly two tons of gun with its aerodynamic drag. The centerline mounting pylon wasn't designed to adsorb the massive recoil generated by cannon fire. The pod flexed during firing, adversely affecting accuracy. The F-4C and F-4D models didn't have trajectory-predicting gunsights which would have shown the pilot where the stream of lead would be going. So, in the immortal words of René Fonck, French WWI flying ace, "The only solution for a maneuvering target is point-blank range." Still, 1200 rounds at 100 rounds a second produced impressive firepower. Observe 12 seconds on your watch or phone while imaging 100 rounds of high explosive cannon shells departing your aircraft every second and heading in the general vicinity of the target. I once flew a F-4D with three, count 'em, three, gun pods, one on the centerline with one on each wing. Now that was a stream of hot lead, 300 rounds a second!

True to form, the insular US Navy tech team ignored the had-earned lessons of the USAF gun pod while developing their own version. They employed a different, slower-firing 20 mm gun in a pod for naval F-4Bs. It turned out to be even worse, with all the drawbacks of the USAF lash-up with none of its (limited) effectiveness. The naval gun pod was known by naval aviators as a "single-shot" device as it usually jammed after one or two rounds.

Despite wing's fearsome nickname, the 366th never shot down any MiGs with the Vulcan gun pod. Only my squadron, the 433rd, notched gun kills of airborne targets with the F-4D. The Da Nang "Gunfighter" wing's three squadrons used the centerline cannon for close air support if at all. It wasn't popular with pilots in combat regardless of its cartoon rendering on the wing's distinctive shoulder patch.

Close air support, particularly with troops in contact with the enemy was, and still is, a demanding mission requiring precision ordnance delivery. Fighter pilots usually worked with a Forward Air Controller, a FAC, flying a tiny light plane such as a single-engine O-1 Bird Dog (a militarized Cessna C-180). Later in the war, they flew the O-2, a military version of the Cessna Skymaster with two engines mounted in a push/pull configuration.

The FAC would talk the fighters into seeing the target area, specifying where everyone was located on the ground in the battlespace. Using shallow dive angles and low release altitudes, fighters attempted to rain death and destruction on the heads of the Viet Cong or North Vietnamese regular army troops while leaving the "friendlies," the Good Guys, untouched and un-bombed. A single mistake could ruin a career and leave an errant fighter pilot with life-long nightmares of killing allies, even Americans.

After a brief stop at Clark AB, PI, I reported to Da Nang ready to return to the war and the skies over Vietnam only to learn I must attend "New Guys' School." This scheduled five days of lectures intended to acquaint personnel new to the theatre with the local ropes. We finished on a Friday afternoon. Pilots in the New Guys' class were told to report to the office of the Wing Director of Operations, the Wing DO's, office for a welcoming talk. This led to one of the most unique meetings I ever attended in the USAF, one I can't forget no matter how hard I try.

People new to a squadron were usually in-briefed and welcomed by the Squadron Commander or Operations Officer, sometimes in an office, sometimes in the crew room. A first meeting conducted at the O Club bar wasn't unknown. Seldom would such an exalted functionary like the Wing DO conduct such a confab with low-ranking junior officers.

We three "newbies" were ushered into the Wing DO's inner sanctum. After saluting, we were seated in chairs in front of his desk. I wasn't in a mood to be welcomed. I just spent a week of my max 52-week combat tour listening to boring lectures such as the one from a Flight Surgeon on how to avoid contracting Sexually Transmitted Diseases, STDs, with the local girls, Vietnamese and "round-eyes" alike. I already knew that.

The DO, a full Colonel, sat behind a totally clean and bare desk. I later learned while working in the defense industry to distrust executives with clean desks. The DO represented a kind of a senior executive for the fighter wing but his desk was as barren as the Sahara Desert only without the sand dunes and camels. This could have meant one of several things; 1) He didn't have enough to do, 2) A case of Obsessive-Compulsive Disorder, OCD, 3) He was a neat freak, or 4) All of the above.

The actual diagnosis was worse.

Without the customary pleasantries such as "It's great to have you guys here" the DO began his talk. He stressed the need to follow rules and procedures and the proper way USAF officers were to conduct themselves on- or off-base. He then launched into a tirade driven by one over-arching idea. He stressed no pilot in the wing should consider himself to be better than any other jock. No squadron could collectively think they were better than either of the other two F-4 units on base. He would not put up with any rivalry or competition between pilots, aircrews, or squadrons. He finished with, "Dismissed." No questions allowed. We stood, saluted, did about-faces, and split. Welcome to Da Nang.

On the walk back to my new squadron, I did a quick analysis of this abysmal situation. Fighter pilots are *uber*-competitive. It is in our genes. Whether at the squadron ping-pong table, the pool room, or airborne during ACM training, we compete, hard. Indeed, air-to-air combat with MiGs is the ultimate "*mano-y-mano*" competition, now sometimes *senora-*

y-mano. It pays to have the right competitive mindset ingrained for success and/or survival.

I recognized the DO for what he was, and more importantly, what he wasn't. The good colonel undoubtedly spent years climbing the rank ladder after a short initial flying assignment. He had prospered, had been promoted, had won awards, all for diligent staff work. He was cited for writing papers, for attending all the right professional service schools, and for shining at various, non-flying, headquarters assignments. An accomplished paper-pusher, he was sent to Da Nang to check the box for a "combat" tour in SEA, a vital requirement for further promotion, likely to be at the Pentagon. He would fly once a week, maybe, with an IP in the rear cockpit on the day's easiest mission and never at night. A Distinguished Flying Cross medal would be his for some forgettable, routing mission. He would be awarded an Air Medal, the USAF equivalent of a Little League participation trophy. He would someday be a general. He would never be a fighter pilot.

Senior officers of fighter wings occupy unique positions in the US military. No one expects a US Army battalion commander to walk point on a jungle patrol. No captain of a US Navy ship handles the helm in heavy seas. But a Wing Commander, or a DO, is expected to fly the same missions in the same aircraft as the most junior jet jockey, preferably while leading a formation. I couldn't see the DO of the Gunfighters leading the wing, or the Wolfpack.

Even back then, I could see the DO was riven by insecurity. He knew he would never be able to lead or to earn respect from squadron jocks, particularly *prima-donnas* like me. He found himself responsible for the actions of a motley crew of fighter pilots whose ability to cause official trouble remained legendary. All it would take would be for one stick of bombs to land on the friendlies, one dumb-assed aircraft accident, one bar fight in Da Nang City, one major security violation, and his cherished climb up the chain of command would be terminated. He knew he couldn't lead by example so he chose to lead by issuing orders against competition. Thus, he thought, to keep the lid on. All I could think of was, "How do I get out of this chickenshit outfit?" Any military unit, be it a wing or a squadron, reflects the personality and the *nous* of the its leadership. I wanted no part of the Da Nang wing nor its so-called leaders.

Back at the squadron, I got on the military phone network and called Ubon. I was able to reach my previous flight commander, who was still there, to ask if he needed my help. As a GIB, I had been heavily involved in the Laser-Guided Bomb, LGB, program. The 433rd TFS had been chosen to introduce these wonder-weapons from the future to today's aerial warfare. We also introduced these terminally-guided bombs to the North Vietnamese much to their sorrow. Major Brad Sharp told me the LGB results had recently gone south and to call back in two hours. I did. Sharp said, "Yes, we can use your expertise with LGBs. We think we can get you assigned back to the 433rd."

That's all the permission I needed. I packed my government-issued suitcase, a "B-4" bag, gathered my flight gear from the Personal Equipment shop, took my name off the next day's flying schedule (It would have been my first sortie at Da Nang), and pitched up at the aerial port squadron. Military transfers were done with written orders, without fail. Transport on military cargo aircraft required valid orders. I had none, but I talked myself onboard a US Marine C=130 Hercules aircraft bound for Ubon. The Marines didn't care if I flashed orders or not.

The next day, I checked into the 433^{rd,} same flight, same hooch, as eight months before. The day after that I flew a combat sortie dropping LGBs. No New Guys' School. The orders authorizing my transfer from Da Nang to Ubon caught up with me two weeks later.

As mentioned earlier, my combat experience at Ubon with the Wolfpack and with Satan's Angles is chronicled in another book. Now would be a good time to read *War for the Hell of It*.

CHAPTER TEN
NELLIS AFB, LAS VEGAS, NV. 1972

What Happens in Vegas, Gets Taught Elsewhere.

The 414th Fighter Weapons Squadron, FWS, at Nellis AFB, outside North Las Vegas, NV. offered fighter pilots a graduate degree in weapons and tactics. Somehow, I managed to wrangle an assignment there. But why was this assignment a good idea and how did it happen?

The Fighter Weapons School trained instructors, IPs, in the latest tactics, weapons, and fighter plane operations. Pilots known as "good sticks" for being adept were sent to the FWS from their home squadrons for an intensive four-month school of instruction and flight operations. Then each returned to his unit to spread the word. I first became aware of what these graduates could do when my F-4 upgrade squadron at MacDill AFB, FL counted Captain Walt Radiker as its resident FWS graduate. Walt knew everything. He could explain it all in exhaustive, and exhausting, detail. You didn't ask him anything about fighter operations unless you had 20-30 minutes to listen. I stood in awe of such a knowledgeable FWS IP.

During the Vietnam War, the FWS periodically sent senior instructors from the school to SEA to catch up on the latest thinking and combat operations in order to incorporate that info into the FWS curriculum. In the early 1970's word started to filter back to Nellis that something big was happening in the field, and in the sky, with terminally-guided munitions.

Historically, the combat operations of guided air-to-ground bombs represented an activity unblemished by success. Radio-controlled drones loaded with high explosives were tried as early as WWI. An obsolete biplane would be crammed with dynamite to be remotely controlled by a pilot in another biplane. That didn't work. The same idea was tried in

WWII with remotely flown B-17s with little improvement over the WWI biplanes. The Germans achieved some success with radio-controlled bombs against anchored Italian battleships, hardly challenging targets. In the US air forces, we tried various means of reducing those quarter-mile combat CEPs including glide bombs steered by pigeons. I am not making this up. Nothing seemed to work, the technology and the pigeons, weren't capable of executing the mission. After Korea, the USAF deployed the command-guided Bullpup missile. This was a rocket-propelled bomb steered with a tiny control stick mounted in a fighter cockpit just aft of the throttles. The intrepid pilot needed to fly his own aircraft with his right hand and fly the bomb to target impact with his left at the same time. That didn't work so well either. As with the biplanes and the B-17s, it's hard enough to fly one plane and very difficult to fly two.

The US Navy went down a different track. They developed and deployed a glide bomb with a TV camera in its nose. Using his cockpit radar display as a TV set, the pilot, or the GIB, or the B/N (Bombardier/Navigator in the USN) would lock the TV onto the target and release the weapon. The Walleye, as it was called, would fly to keep the target scene centered on its own TV until impact. This launch-and-leave device worked better than the Bullpup, and the pigeons, but required much aircrew training, clear weather, and an isolated and TV-friendly target. Designed to take out bridges, the round was too expensive to employ on routine targets such as trucks and gun emplacements.

Inter the Laser Guided Bomb, the LGB. This was a low-cost guidance kit screwed onto the front of a standard "dumb" bomb warhead making it a "smart bomb." The laser seeker on the bomb didn't need to know where the target was or what it was. It only had to fly to a tiny laser spot shining on the ground, like a pussy cat chasing a laser pointer. The laser illumination was provided by a GIB from the back seat of a second F-4. One Phantom would drop two bombs while his wingman illuminated the target Then the two aircrews would trade roles. This worked great. The 433rd TFS at Ubon was chosen to combat-test the LGB concept and the associated hardware. There were many days when the 433rd was credited with more targets destroyed than the rest of the out-country USAF squadrons in SEA. We could pick off targets at will from high altitude, keeping our pink asses out of the ground fire.

Finally, we had a successful way to reduce CEPs to near zero. Each LGB, baring some monumental screw-up, would hit withing ten feet of the laser spot shining on the ground. I flew many back-seat LGB missions and upon my somewhat unorthodox return to the 433rd from Da Nang, many more in the front cockpit. LGB's were cheap and effective.

However, combat from medium altitude is still combat. Every mission carried with it the risk of being shot down, killed, or captured by the Bad Guy. We all hoped we would never need to use our survival and resistance training. Sadly, some of us were unlucky enough to do just that.

When I began this book, I asked my 433rd squadron mate and friend, Bill Schwertferger, call sign "Shortfinger," to comment on the effectiveness of our survival training after he was shot down and captured in NVN. Bill spent over a year as a POW in the infamous "Hanoi Hilton." His reply was fascinating for two reasons; the requested comment about survival training, but also as an account of how serious the North Vietnamese feared LGBs. I decided to include Bill's input verbatim, below.

* * *

I was asked by my friend, Fast Eddie Cobleigh, a fellow 433rd Satan's Angel and 414th FWS Instructor, to discuss my survival training lessons learned and how they applied to my time as a Prisoner of War, POW, held in Hanoi from 16 February 72 until 28 March 73.

I graduated from pilot training in September 1968, getting a backseat F-4 assignment and then went to Water Survival School at Homestead AFB, Fl. There I learned how to survive an overwater ejection. Overall, a pretty good school. In November 1968, I went to Fairchild AFB, WA for the USAF Survival School. Unfortunately, our class was the last class for the Winter to go deep into the snow covered Mountains. The trek portion was wasted, as we were enroute to the jungles of SEA. While at the main school, following the trek, I learned somethings about POWs, interrogations, good guy/bad guy, and a little about coping with solitary confinement.

I then went to the F-4 RTU at George AFB, CA and then to special weapons training at Nellis AFB, NV. From there, I went to Clark AFB, PI, for Jungle Survival School. A better school aimed at teaching me about how to survive in the jungle environment and how to avoid capture. It was almost impossible to hide from the local natives in the PI.

I arrived at Ubon RTAB, Thailand, the 8th TFW, 433rd TFS in August 69 and returned to the States in June 70 for upgrade to the F-4's front seat and returned to the 8th TFW, 433rd TFS in April 71 after receiving special weapons training again at Nellis, AFB, NV. During both combat tours, I flew 150 sorties as a Laser Guided Bomb, LGB, Guy In Back, GIB. After 200 missions, as a handed-picked GIB & pilot of the Wolf FACs (Forward Air Controllers). Most of my sorties were flown over Laos with maybe 30 over North Vietnam, as Protective Reaction Strikes. In the later part of my second tour, I started carrying four hand grenades and six loaded hollow-point bullets in my 38 pistol. The reasoning was based upon the Laotians were not taking captives but rather chopping the crews heads off with machetes.

During my 350 combat missions, my aircraft was hit at total of 7 times, of which I was able to return to home base on 6 of them.

16 February 1972, I was shot down over North Vietnam, north of the DMZ, by a Soviet-lead team firing the first ever SA-2F (Optically-Guided Surface to Air Missile (SAM). I was immediately captured in the corner of a rice paddy by a dozen NVN regulars coming up each side of the dike. The lead soldier, on my left was firing his 9mm pistol and striking the water at my feet. I looked at my hand grenades and had a discussion with the "Duke" above as to whether to pulls the pins and go out in a blaze of glory or live to fight another day. The Duke looked down and said, "Shortfinger, discretion is the better part of valor, live to fight another day," and so I did.

My back seater, Lt Ralph Galati, (RG), and myself were held overnight in a bunker and then driven to Hanoi the next day. We arrived late at night on the 17th and was immediately separated in solitary rooms for integrations. On the way to Hanoi, I told RG that we were on our very first mission of local orientation and got lost and shot down. WE DO NOT KNOW ANYTHING! Stick with it!

I would spend 90 days in Solitary confinement and constantly quizzed about Laser Guided Systems. I repeatedly claimed ignorance and said I did not know about this system. In one instance, there were Caucasians with blue epaulets in the back of the room (possible Russians). Even when the Vietnamese laid out an Aviation Week magazine in front of me, I said, "You best read the article because I do not know a thing about this system." Always going back to on my first mission and being lost. As I looked around the room and saw the hooks in the roof and side rafters, I thought about all those who had been tortured and beaten and dropped from those hooks. The only thing that gave me confidence was the little guy doing the interrogations was obviously told to keep his hands off me. I also prayed the Rosary during each integration to keep my mind off them. In May, I was put in a solitary cell with RG. He had said that the Vietnamese had no interest in him and had left him pretty much alone. While in solitary, we learned the tap code (5x5 without the K) and hand signing to communicate with the old guys across the courtyard.

On 10 May, I was removed from my cell and dragged out the front gate to a waiting jeep. I told myself this is going to be really different. I was taken to a completely different camp and thrown in to a room with a Vietnamese we called the "Bug" and with "Straps & Bars," a known torture team. His very first question was about LGB's. As I said, I Do Not---a rifle butt hit me in my right temple and sent me to the ground. Dazed, I got back up to hear in a screaming voice,

"TELL ME ABOUT LGBS." I again started with I and the Bug motions to Straps & Bars to throw me to the ground and then to tie me in a modified ropes torture that almost dislocated by left shoulder and cut the blood supply to my arms, legs, and internal organs. Now I was looking up my own self in a ball and the Bug screams and spits, "TELL ME ABOUT LGBS." I was gasping for air and really unable to say much but I said, "I do not.." The Bug went berserk and has Straps & Bars get a 6' fan belt from a big diesel truck so he could whip me into submission. Upon seeing that, I say I might know something but could not breathe or talk very well. They wait and finally remove the ropes. The pain coming out was tremendous with blood flowing back into my arms, legs, back, and internal organs.

Back at the Hilton, I sent another 2 weeks in solitary confinement with around the clock interrogations. The first quiz following the ropes, I started out with I don't know and the Vietnamese laid out a copy of my AF form 5 (the squadron flight log) from the 433rd, the laser squadron, showing all my time working with the systems. Now caught, I had to talk in circles about what the LGBs system could not really do. In the meantime, I'm teaching new guys the tap code, the hand sign codes, and the camp Rules of Engagement, ROE, laid down by Robbie Risner and Will Stockdale; take torture to the point of loss of limb or life. I finally signed the biggest lie about LGBs by transforming the letters T & F in my last name, thus showing that it was made under torture.

I later found out that on the 10th of May 72, Captain Roger Locher was shot down over Thud Ridge by a pair of MiG 19s. Their mission was a blocking force to keep MiGs from making it to Thanh Wah Bridge while the Navy was blocking from the coast inland to Keep the MiGs away. This was all to protect the 8th TFW, 433rd Satan's Angels, LGB bombers as they dropped the bridge. A feat never done in 8 years. That's why they took the gloves off and tortured me on 10 May.

After I returned to a community cell with my fellow new guys, I continued to be defiant with the Vietnamese, to write letters home, and being a part of the camp communications team.

Bill "Shortfinger" Schwertfeger
USAF, LTC, Ret
3 Silver Stars, 4 DFC's, 36 Air Medals, Bronze Star w/V, 2 Purple Hearts and POW Medal.

* * *

Some further explanations might be helpful. The tap code was a 5x5 matrix of the alphabet used to tap audible messages through the Hanoi Hilton's walls. A POW would tap pairs of numbers indicating which letters were being sent. Colonel Robby Risner, USAF, and Captain Will Stockdale, USN, were the senior POWs in rank. They assumed command of the "1st POW Wing, Provisional" as required by the Uniform Code of Conduct taught in survival schools. As a result of the lessons learned in the Hanoi Hilton, the code has been amended to be more workable and less rigid. Originally, the code limited information given by a US POW to name, rank, service number, and date of birth. This approach worked if we were fighting other western countries such as Germany or Italy which tended to follow the same code. When pilots were captured by the armed forces of countries much less concerned with the obligations of civilized behavior in war, such as Korea, North Vietnam, and Iraq, the code broke down. Also, during the early days of the Vietnam War, many American aviators were shot down and captured. During the time the LBJ administration was trying to mollify the Bad Guys by calling bombing halts, not so many were added to the roster in the Hanoi Hilton.

These early POWs were the "old guys" Bill mentioned. Some were captive for over seven years. When President Nixon decided to take the gloves off and blow the shit out of North Vietnam with B-52s, more POWs were captured. These are the "new guys."

The Thanh Wah Bridge mission will be covered in more exciting details later in this book.

The USAF brain trust didn't know about the Bad Guys' fixation on LGBs but did know the system worked well. The then-current techniques of LGB delivery were not well known at the FWS. Lt Col Bill Wilson was dispatched to SEA as part of the ongoing curriculum update. Wilson pitched up at Ubon. He was put on the flight schedule for a LGB mission. I was the flight leader. That was an ego trip. Here was me, a junior captain, with the FWS Operations Officer as my wingman. If there was ever a time not to screw up, that was surely it.

I briefed the mission in detail, educating Bill Wilson on the subtleties of LGB delivery. The target for that day was a cluster of 37mm Anti-Aircraft, AA, guns. AA guns existed for one reason, to shoot down our aircraft and kill or capture our pilots. Each gun presented a difficult target, dug into a deep revetment, maybe 30 feet across, with tall circular earthen berms protecting the gun and its crew. Near misses by dumb bombs were ineffective. Given the wide CEPs, getting an unguided bomb inside a revetment was almost impossible. To date, the only solution had been cluster bombs. If you could place one baseball-sized bomblets inside the gun position, it would silence the gun for a time. But it was easy to see from the ground when a cluster bomb cannister opened. The gun crew would take temporary shelter in a bunker recessed into in the revetment. To make matters worse, delivery of dumb bombs or cluster bombs required the fighter aircraft to dive directly at the gun at low altitude. This solved the gunners' tracking problem as their target, us, was not traversing across the sky, only getting bigger in their gunsights.

Bill Wilson put two 2000-pound bombs into two 37mm gun emplacements, releasing the LGBs at the relatively safe altitude of 12,000 feet, out of the guns' effective range. 2000-pound bombs, whose blast and fragmentation was confined and focused inside the revetments, obliterated the guns and everyone associated with the piece. What was two neatly constructed gun emplacements were violently converted into smoking craters. There is some primal, savage satisfaction in vaporizing people who are doing their level best to kill you.

Lt Col Wilson returned to the FWS, preaching with the passion of the newly converted, of the need to establish better LGB training. A separate cadre of IPs was designated as the Terminal Guided Weapons Flight and stocked with 433rd TFS alumni, including me, once I finished my combat tour. Evidently, Bill Wilson liked what he saw when I led him in combat with LGBs. He returned to Nellis and requested me by name for the 414th TG Flight members/instructors did not have to be FWS graduates. However, the fickle finger of fate solved that omission problem for me.

One of the incoming students in a new FWS class, after a Saturday night of drinking at the Officers Club, wrapped his Porsche around a telephone pole. The poor guy was looking at some months of hospital care and rehab. This left an opening, a vacant slot, in the next class with no time to request a replacement from the field. Sunday, I got a call that I was to start the Weapons School the next day.

This was like a good baseball player at the AAA level getting a text from his manager informing him that he was going to The Show, the Major League team, tomorrow. I was fortunate that the interval was so short. I didn't have time to get twitched about starting in the majors. Sometimes it's just as good to be lucky as to be good. Some of us were unlucky.

This year, Tom Reasor, a classmate in UPT class 68B died when his B-52 bomber crashed at Utapao Royal Thai Air Force Base in Thailand on the Gulf of Siam. The giant craft was heavily damaged, with multiple engines on the same side out, on a strike on North Vietnam during Operation Linebacker II. The aircraft commander lost control on touchdown and the B-52 rolled and disintegrated.

Rich Long, another classmate in 68B, was killed when his privately-owned Mooney light aircraft ran out of gas. It was an ironic end for a guy whose USAF career in KC-135 tankers was spent making sure other pilots had enough fuel. Rich's ambition was to fly for the airlines, hence his choice of assignments. He never made it.

CHAPTER ELEVEN
FIGHTER WEAPONS SCHOOL, 1972

Welcome to The Show

Flight operations at the FWS were the most intense, the most action-packed, the most demanding I ever experienced outside of actual combat. The FWS IPs observed, graded, and critiqued every phase of a flight from the initial pre-flight briefing until the final, post-flight debrief. We students not only had to fly difficult missions but we also had to demonstrate that we could critique and teach others as well.

The school was broken down into three phases: air-to-air combat, nuclear weapons delivery, and air-to-ground weapons employment. The FWS had two adjunct flights; the Terminal Guided Weapons Flight and the Wild Weasel Flight (concerned with electronic and missile suppression of enemy defenses) both were not part of the core FWS curriculum. The TG and Wild Weasel flights provided only introductory classroom introduction to their specialties with no dedicated flights..

A typical day began with a flight briefing, sometimes as early as 0600, and ended with classroom academics until late in the afternoon. Each FWS instructor was also a platform professor lecturing and testing in his specialty. Perhaps the hardest lesson was how to put aside your ego, first to learn, then to teach. Fighter pilots are rumored to be highly competitive. However, when correcting a student's mistake, it wasn't cool to remark, "You screwed that maneuver up because you are not as good as I am." You had to guide the student to self-realization.

However, when a particularly awful mission unfolded, fire and brimstone rained down on the hapless jock. After a really bad day, Bill Wilson chewed me out, but good. He probably wondered why he ever tapped me for the squadron. I left work early, driving home before my wife and daughter arrived. Locking myself in the garage, I cried, cursing the day I was born. Then and there, I vowed to show that SOB I could lead a flight correctly.

Another challenge was to keep up with your fellow students, who were sent to the school because of their demonstrated expertise. Graduation from the FWS was a career-building step. Several of my classmates went on to higher rank and to command wings later in their USAF lives. Wearing the FWS graduate patch on your flight suit was mandatory, replacing any lesser patch. One of my classmates, Dick Myers, went on to be Chairman of the Joint Chiefs of Staff, the highest-ranking military officer in the US, as a four-star general. Even at that exhalated level, whenever he wore a flight suit, he proudly displayed his FWS patch. Dick is one of the good guys. He is a general officer who never let the stars on his shoulders go to his head.

Finally, I graduated, a FWS IP. I believe I was the youngest instructor in the history of the FWS. I was the only one who went through the school then stayed on in the 414th. My friend and squadron mate Brigadier General Steve Ritchie, the USAF ace with five air-to-air kills in SEA, says he was the youngest. I have never called him on it as the claim is part of his branding, important for his gigs as a public speaker. But, if Steve ever asks, I have the birth certificate and the orders to prove it. He wants the title more than I do.

Each Weapons School class ended with a "turkey shoot." This was a bombing competition on a scored gunnery range located at Indian Spring Air Force Station, now Creech AFB, NV. Both students and IPs competed. Somehow, my (unguided) ordnance found its way close enough to the target. I won the Turkey Shoot, defeating my classmates and squadron mates. As the scores were being posted, Bill Wilson commented to the Squadron Commander, Lt/Col Larry Armstrong, "Looks like we got a good one.' I'm sure Wilson felt justified in going to bat for me. As baseball great Dizzy Dean said, "It ain't bragging if you can do it."

After graduation, I returned to the TG flight continuing to preach the gospel of guided weapons. For the FWS students, I distilled my academic presentations on TG weapons down to a one-hour lesson. This was usually scheduled for 1500 on a Friday afternoon when the FWS students were eager for happy hour at the O Club. They were constantly checking their large fighter pilot wrist watches. The title of my lecture was, "Terminally Guided Weapons; The Wave of the Future." This did not go down well with guys who just spent a month learning the intricacies of fixed-angle dive bombing with dumb bombs.

For the students going through the TG flight's training, I had a lecture on Laser-Guided Bomb Technology, abbreviated as LGBT. Much later, that abbreviation was highjacked for another, unrelated subject. I like to tell folks that as a practicing heterosexual, and I needed the practice, I taught a class on LBGT for the USAF.

Now, nearly all air-to-ground weapons are guided in some manner. Even today, I get emails from guys who went through the 414th FWS. Quite a few mention the "Wave of the Future" lecture by name. They say, "Fast Eddie, we all thought you were a nut, a crank, a wild-eyed fanatic, with that TG bullshit." However, the wave of the future has crested, washing away dumb bombs and horrendous CEPs.

Another strong recommendation for TG weapons is the avoidance of collateral damage. I know for a fact that you can put a TV-guided Maverick missile into a particular apartment house window in Beirut, Lebanon. Squadron mate and friend Hal Rhoden witnessed his Israeli students ace their Maverick employment school final exam. The sea-side flat was where top-ranking official of the Palestine Liberation Organization lived, but not for long. In times past, air strikes would have had to level the entire building along with its residents to achieve the same desired result, death to a single terrorist.

During WWII, German and Japanese cities were carpet-bombed by the Royal Air Force and the US Army Air Force into many square miles of smoking rubble with hundreds of thousands, maybe millions, of civilians losing their lives in the process. Given the inaccuracy of un-guided dumb bombs, all the air forces back then could hit were targets the size of Hamburg or Tokyo, particularly at night. Today, that sort of operation is considered to be a war crime. Unless, of course, the Russians do it. Then it's standard operation procedure. It is ridiculous on some level to think about a more humane way of waging war, but that's what TG weapons have wrought. We no longer need to dump random high explosives all over the place to win. We can take out high-value targets with precision and cause much lower causalities. If I there is one thing I take pride in on my USAF career, it would be my role, however minor, in introducing and preaching the gospel of TG weapons. "The Wave of the Future" indeed.

Despite the raging success of LGBs in SEA, there was one instance when a highly capable TG munition wasn't employed as designed, a failure which had nothing to do with mission effectiveness. As The Bard wrote in *Macbeth,* "Read on, Macduff."

CHAPTER TWELVE
NELLIS AFB, NV. 1972

Nuke Walleye Versus the Dragon's Jaw

The Vietnam War was not going well on the ground or in the air. Over North Vietnam, the Dragon's Jaw was biting hard. It had been devouring American planes and aircrew since 1965. Nobody knew how to pull its teeth. The Thanh Hoa bridge over the Song Ha River, 3 miles (4.8 km) northeast of Thanh Hoa, North Vietnam, carried both rail and road traffic, a key link on the principal route for war supplies flowing south to the Viet Cong. Both sides in the war understood the importance of the bridge as a potential choke point. The North Vietnamese stationed three air defense battalions near the bridge armed with numerous AA guns of all calibers. MiG-17 interceptors were on call in the area as well. By some estimates, 75 US aircraft, including a giant C-130 transport and its 13-man crew, were lost in operations trying to drop the bridge, earning its nickname, The Dragon's Jaw, from the North Vietnamese.

Nothing seemed to work. Squadrons of F-105 Thunderchief fighter-bombers from our bases in Thailand attacked the bridge with 750-pound iron bombs and Bullpup command-guided missiles. Flying off carriers in the Gulf of Tonkin, the US Navy tried Walleye TV-guided glide bombs. USAF C-130 four-engine transports dropped magnetic mines upstream, which floated down river and detonated under the bridge. Scorched, bent, and scarred, the bridge endured, never out of service for more than a few hours. Along with its counterpart, the Paul Doumer Bridge over the Red River linking Hanoi and Haiphong, the Thanh Hoa bridge was an obsession for US planners working the target list in North Vietnam considered politically acceptable by the White House. But, absent a way to sever the steel trusses spanning the river once and for all, additional mass raids, with the inevitable losses, seemed criminally futile and dangerous to the over-stretched aircrews. So the bridge still stood and the war supplies flowed southward.

At the US Navy's Naval Air Weapons Center, China Lake, CA, a group of engineers resolved to come up with a new plan. Accuracy wasn't the major problem; a Walleye's TV guidance system could deliver ordinance to the bridge. Killing the bridge was the challenge. The weapon's 250 pound linear shaped-charge warhead was successful in cutting steel beams and girders in the test arena at China Lake. But, against real bridges like the Dragon's Jaw, not so much. The expanding, steel-cutting shrapnel flew through the mostly open bridge girders without effect. The team urgently needed a new, more powerful warhead for the Walleye.

The weapons wizards at China Lake thought the Los Alamos National Laboratory, north of Albuquerque, NM, might hold the key to fracturing the Dragon's Jaw. Originally developed for the Davy Crockett recoilless rifle system, many W72 nuclear warheads were available. The miniature device was the most tested nuke in the US inventory. Dozens of trials were run, not to increase the explosive yield as with other warheads, but to decrease its destructive power. A short-range nuke deployed by the US Army with the equivalent power of many kilotons of TNT would be like a hand grenade with a 100-foot kill radius and a two second delay, i.e., suicide to deliver from a jeep-mounted recoilless rifle. Eventually, the hellfire yield was dialed down to "only" 20 tons of TNT, .02 kilotons, 1/1000th of the size of the fireballs at Hiroshima and Nagasaki which ended WWII.

The USAF had adapted the tiny nuke warhead for the AIM-4 Falcon air-to-air missile, tasking it to blast whole formations of enemy bombers out of the sky at one go. Warhead power was scaled back up to 400 hundred tons for the Falcon. The atom scientists in New Mexico were confident they could improve the yield to just over six hundred tons using the W72s salvaged from retired Falcon missiles. The equivalent of six hundred tons of TNT would trash any bridge in the world with one weapon delivered by one fighter aircraft.

The cylinder-shaped W72 measured just 10 3/4 inches (27cm) in diameter with hemispherical ends 15 1/2 inches (39 cm) apart and it weighed only 50 pounds (23 kilos). It would slip easily inside the Walleye's tubular body, replacing the heavy conventional warhead. The lighter weight would extend the glide bomb's aerodynamic range. The China Lake team considered the installation of the W72 into their terminally guided munition a marriage made, not in heaven, but in the fires of nuclear hell.

The Walleye had been developed at China Lake. It was the first American terminally guided munition, a "smart bomb," to perform well in combat. The term "smart bomb" came from the different paths different bombs take once released from an aircraft. Dumb bombs only know where the ground is, smart bombs know where the target is.

The glide bomb's nose featured a flattened glass dome with a TV camera staring out through it. Resemblance to a giant fish's eye earned the Walleye its aquatic nickname. Why the China Lake boffins, stuck out in the middle of the Mojave Desert, named their creation after a cold-water member of the pike family from Minnesota remains a mystery. Launched from high altitude, the nuke Walleye could glide over 30 miles with a spinning ram air turbine supplying electrical power. It would hit within a few feet of the aim point. Six hundred tons of explosive power vaporizing the center span of the Thanh Hoa bridge would break the Dragon's Jaw forever. Then the targeters could turn their lethal attention to the Paul Doumer bridge.

Employing the Nuke Walleye would be easy for the aircrews. As with the conventionally armed Walleye, a fighter pilot would set up a shallow dive from high altitude miles from the bridge, out of range for the defenders. He would aim his aircraft to put his gunsight on the general area of the distant bridge. The Walleye's TV camera was bore-sighted to stare at the target under the projected gun sight. A radar screen in the launch aircraft doubled as a black and white TV set displaying the target area as seen by the weapon's sensor. Four-power magnification made target identification easy, not that it would be hard to spot a long bridge. Usually, only a slight change in flight path superimposed the Walleye's aiming crosshairs on the scope over the target to lock the camera on. Once the display had settled down after a second or two, a quick press of the bomb release button, the pickle button, launched the Walleye. The TV guidance system would guide the bomb to a direct hit, homing in on optically contrasting details on the bridge, blackened steel structure silhouetted against a grey-water river.

After the conventional, non-nuke, Walleye left the aircraft, the cockpit TV display went snow white. No further action by the aircrew was needed, or even possible, the bomb was on its own. The launch aircraft was then free to get the hell out of the reach of the Dragon's breath defenses.

Nuke Walleye boasted one additional trick. After launch, the cockpit TV display wouldn't go blank. A video data link would transmit the TV camera's picture back to the aircraft until impact and detonation. The missile was dropped with the warhead in a safe condition. The W72 had to be armed after the aircrew monitoring their TV display determined the bomb was headed for the right target. A second pickle button push would arm the weapon with a signal sent along the data link from the jet to the bomb. A black stripe across the scope signified the arming command had received and that a mini-mushroom cloud would soon blossom. This added step was easier in a two-seat aircraft like the A-6 Intruder or F-4 Phantom. The second crew member, the Bomb/Nav (USN) or the Weapon Systems Operator (USAF), could confirm the aim point and arm the W72 while the pilot kept his attention out of the cockpit, scanning for MiG's or surface-to-air missiles.

What about the effects of a nuclear blast on the area around the bridge? The W72 was not a threat to an unprotected person standing only 3000 feet from ground zero. There would be some collateral damage, but this was judged to be worth the price for not losing any more aircraft, or the war. Basically an air-burst weapon, the nuke would not generate much lingering radiation.

The Nuke Walleye was designed, the components were tested, the aircraft were modified, and aircrews were trained in its use. I can attest to this as I trained the USAF crews. It is unclear from the records if many of the terminally guided, nuclear-armed smart bombs were ever fully assembled. Certainly, none were used. Why not?

American leaders concluded nuclear weapons were not just devices with bigger bangs, but represented an entirely different class of weapon, one reserved for existential national threats, not hard tactical problems. So, the Vietnam War agony dragged on, war material still flowing south over the bridges to kill Americans. But, conventional terminally-guided weapons were improving rapidly. In 1972, 12 F-4's flying from Ubon, Thailand, dropped the Thanh Hoa bridge with 2000-pound Laser-Guided Bombs with laser illumination provided by Pave Knife targeting pods. The LGB's hit within 3 feet of their aim point. The Dragon's Jaw was shattered by the USAF Phantoms, without a single aircraft loss and without summoning the nuclear genie.

The only surviving (unarmed) Nuke Walleye can be seen today in the Atomic Weapons Museum on Kirtland AFB, Albuquerque, NM. To enter the museum, you need a military ID card and to not be pregnant. Other nuclear weapons on display there have some residual radiation.

In the process of training the nuke walleye aircrews for the USAF, I visited the weapons center in Albuquerque to gain as much knowledge as I could for the FWS tactics manual I was writing. The technical team was proud of what they had wrought and were very helpful. They explained to me the nuke walleye employed a unique mechanical arming device used in the detonation of the warhead. This gizmo was called a "Rollamite inertial switch." It consisted of a roller constrained by a flexible metal strap. When the weapon experienced sudden deacceleration, such as when hitting a bridge, the roller moved at a fixed rate from one end of a matchbox-sized container to the other closing an electrical circuit and setting off the W72 nuke. The guys were very proud of this invention. They claimed the switch was the first completely new mechanical device to be invented in the last 3000 years. They ranked it up there with the inclined plane, the lever, and the wheel. Well, maybe. With my undergraduate degree in Mechanical Engineering, I had my doubts about their claim to enduring fame. I said nothing however. It doesn't pay to provoke nuclear scientists who can prove a man to be an oaf with a flick of their pocket calculators.

Every-proud, the technical staff gave me a larger-scale model of their switch to use as a training aid. This was a metal box about the size of a deck of cards with one Plexiglas side displaying how the roller worked. Thanking them, I threw the model into my briefcase and left for the Albuquerque airport to catch my flight back to Sin City. Going through airport security, I laid my briefcase on the conveyor belt and watched it as it traveled slowly along to the metal detector. Too late, I remembered the training aid. I expected the following scenario to erupt at any second. The gal operating the scanner would spot the metal box, stop the conveyor, open my briefcase, and ask;

"So, what is this?"

My reply, "It's the triggering device for an atom bomb."

Thankfully, the model attracted no attention from the security staff. Nuke walleye never felled the Dragon's Jaw bridge but it nearly blew up my Air Force career. Trying to take a nuke trigger through airport security would have done just that.

CHAPTER THIRTEEN
NELLIS AFB RANGES. 1973

A Non-Combat Loss

The phone call came in at 0200. Calls arriving at two o'clock in the morning are never good news and this one was no exception. It told me FWS IP Bill "Admiral" Nelson and his student, Larry "Cajun" Libertore, had crashed on the Nellis gunnery range during a night ground attack sortie. There were no emergency radio beacons heard by the wingman and no parachutes were sighted. The voice on the other end of the land line held no hope for survivors. I found myself appointed to the accident investigation team. I was ordered to report to Base Operations at dawn for a helicopter ride out to the crash site.

Most of the southern triangle of the State of Nevada is off-limits to civilian personnel. In this wide expanse of high desert are tactical gunnery ranges, restricted airspace for air-to-air training, the Groom Lake airfield - the legendary Area 51 where secret aircraft are based and flown, and the nuclear weapons test site. It is desolate place of sagebrush, dry lakes, barren mountains, rocky canyons, nuclear craters, and death.

After I hung up the phone and explained the sad situation to Pat, my wife, I buried my face in my pillow and beat my fists on the headboard. Losses in combat are wrenching and traumatic but are always expected. One becomes somewhat numb to the carnage, not letting the sadness get to you, or else you can't function in combat yourself. Loss of life in peacetime training is different. It's personal, and intensely affecting. That is not supposed to happen, but it does, all too often.

After a half-hour chopper ride, me and the rest of the core accident team made up of pilots, all officers, arrived at a scene the likes of which I never experienced and one I hope to never see again. The medical troops from the base hospital had been busy collecting the mangled remains of the two pilots and assembling them into piles for sorting, examination, body-bagging, and eventual return to the respective next-of-kin. I saw a naked foot, severed at the ankle, a column of bloody vertebra, various unidentifiable bits of flesh and other terrible things which even now I can't bring myself to picture nor to describe.

I threw up. Then I went to work.

When a fighter aircraft crashes hitting the ground at a shallow dive angle, it usually smears along the ground in a fiery path, shedding parts as it goes until the wreckage comes to a stop in a funeral pyre of burning jet fuel and exploding ammunition. If the doomed plane impacts in a steep dive, the result is a crater ten or more feet deep and 30 or 40 feet across filled with bits of metal and smoldering wreckage. The impact in front of me presented none of those classic characteristics. After a quick look around to make sure no body parts of our friends were unaccounted for, we examined the center of the scattered debris field. It took about ten minutes to determine exactly what happened. We could have written the formal accident report then and there. But rigid bureaucratic protocols must be followed and a detailed investigation must be conducted, no matter how obvious things looked to us at the crash site.

Looking over the debris field, I was struck with how silent the desert seemed once the idling helicopter shut down. No bird songs, no traffic noise, no aircraft overhead; the few humans there spoke softly, almost in reverential whispers. The peace and quiet offered a stark contrast to the horrific explosion which rocked the sagebrush and sands the previous night. Even the barren, desolate mountains ringing the crash site seemed to echo the silence back to us, if indeed silence can be said to echo.

Once again, the thought entered my head, "They almost made it." The Phantom pancaked into the ground with little vertical velocity. Clearly visible, imprinted on the sand, were impressions left by the nose, the wingtips, the engines, and the horizontal stabilators-the tail planes. The F4 slid along for 10-20 feet then rebounded, bounced back into the air as if grasping for one last chance at flight. Then the aircraft exploded. A fireball scattered bits of the plane and its pilots over several acres of desert. All that remained was titanium and aluminum confetti to be gathered up by the crash recovery team.

When we had seen all we could stand, the newly-formed accident investigation team decided, without looking each other in the eyes, to return to the base by helo. There the Chief of Safety gave us our marching orders. We were to thoroughly investigate every possible cause for the crash. Our conclusions were not to be influenced by rank, position, politics, nor personal axes to be ground. We were to let the chips fall where they may to determine if changes needed to be made to prevent a re-occurrence. Despite the obvious nature of the event, the complete process took three weeks of 10-hour days, seven-day weeks. The aircraft didn't have a history of flight control problems. The weather rang clear on the night of the crash. Both crewmembers were well-rested although Bill Nelson had worked in the squadron office most of the afternoon. Bill Wilson said he monitored the pre-flight briefing and noted no omissions.

The target had been a simulated convoy, a line of junk trucks parked along a dirt road bladed into the desert and crossing a fake bridge. It simulated the Ho Chi Minh Trail without the jungle cover, training for the then-current war in SEA. The desert convoy foretold of wars in the Middle East which lay in the future although no one involved knew it at the time. Flare deployment by the wingman effectively lit up the scene. Then a F4 Phantom hit the ground pulling out of a dive-bomb run. We could only speculate on the cause. Mis-reading the altimeter, too low a roll-in altitude, wrong target elevation, lack of crew-coordination, all these were possibilities with no data to eliminate any. All we could say was dive bombing at night in the mountains is inherently dangerous, a blinding flash of the obvious. I resisted the temptation to point out that TG weapons could have eliminated the need to dive toward the unseen ground. That wave of the future had not yet formed. The US Navy safety bureaucracy maintains that there are no accidents, no acts of God, everything has a cause including crashes. Maybe, but sometimes the causes die with the aircrews.

Our report was accepted and forwarded up the chain of command. I can honestly say we were not pressured by anyone to change anything in our findings. Sadly, that mindset seems no longer operative in the USAF safety community.

The F-22 Raptor air superiority fighter has been one of the most politically controversial aircraft ever designed and built. It generated both rabid opposition and fanatical support in the US government. The USAF needed 888 airframes but got only 187 due to politics too arcane to recount here. One of the most controversial aspects of the F-22 procurement has been the pilot's oxygen system.

Until the F-22, USAF aircraft carried bottles of liquid oxygen, lox, for breathing. The lox supply logistics train was extensive and expensive with lox plants, supply trucks, safety considerations, crewing needs. However expensive, the system worked. The people designing the F-22 had an idea to eliminate all that lox infrastructure and save heaps of money. The Raptor separates pure oxygen from air compressed by the engines and pipes it to the cockpit. The system is the On-Board Oxygen Generation System, OBOGS. It almost works. The system has been a source of never-ending problems, particularly after it migrated into other aircraft, including trainers and fighters.

Whenever there is a problem with the OBOGS, a key phrase is used by the safety bureaucracy to describe the problems reported by the pilots; "The aircrew experienced hypoxia-like symptoms." Hypoxia is a medical condition causing mental confusion, lethargy, poor decision-making, and if carried to extremes, unconsciousness. There are only two causes of hypoxia: #1 excessive alcohol consumption, and #2 Lack of breathing oxygen. In the case of US pilots flying military aircraft, I think we can eliminate cause #1. With that, the only source of hypoxia-like symptoms is, ...wait for it...hypoxia. Note the weasel wording, "hypoxia-like symptoms," terminology trying to fuzz up the issue and possibly deflect blame which should attach to a malfunctioning OBOGS.

The most flagrant of inter-service politics warping an accident report occurred in Alaska. An F-22 piloted by Major Jeff Haney crashed in a near-vertical dive at supersonic speed at night. The formal accident report listed the cause of the fatal crash as a failure to maintain aircraft control. The brass essentially blamed the pilot for the crash, who being permanently dead, wasn't there to defend himself. Buried in the bowels of the report lay the details showing the reason the pilot couldn't maintain aircraft control. He couldn't breathe. His OBOGS generated a "sensation similar to suffocation." Note again the weasel wording. Also, his emergency oxygen system required a 50-pound pull with one hand to function. Inflight data showed he was unconscious for 12-15 seconds during the fatal dive. When the aircraft descended low enough, he regained consciousness and tried to pull out. He didn't almost make it. Evidently, it was thought at the higher levels in the Pentagon to be safer to blame the dead pilot than to admit that a well-known problem with the OBOGS had not been fixed, yet.

Despite this white-washed accident report, the F-22 eventually was grounded for several months when two pilots refused to fly it until the root causes of "hypoxia-like" or "similar to suffocation" symptoms were identified and fixed. The Raptor was the ultimate desirable fighter assignment. For pilots to rebel, to stand down in fear of their lives, when fighter pilots are known to be fearless, was extraordinary. Due to investigative reporting by the *60 Minutes* TV show and an outcry raised by the Haney family, the situation received even more attention. The USAF refused to re-examine the accident and stood by the ridiculous conclusion reached in the accident report. I wonder if anyone ever calculated the savings earned by eliminating the lox infrastructure and compared that number to the cost of losing an irreplaceable F-22 Raptor. I'll bet Jeff Haney's family would like to see the same data.

While eliminating the lox infrastructure saved big bucks, the loss of the lox plant did crimp operations on and around the base. No longer could we use lox to "burn" off warts, to freeze grapes, or to ignite charcoal bar-b-ques. But I digress.

The problems with politics intruding into Air Force operations reared its ugly head with me personally, as shown in the next chapter. Fortunately, no one lost their life. I could breathe throughout the episode, although rather quickly and through clenched teeth.

CHAPTER FOURTEEN
LAS VEGAS, NV. 1973

The Night I Met Howard Hughes, Sort Of

Junior captains such as I were tasked periodically at Nellis AFB to be the "Aerodrome Officer" or AO, a job title carried over from WWI when air bases, flying fields with emphasis on "fields" were named "aerodromes." As the lowest ranking officer in the 414th, I pulled this duty often. The duties of the AO were simple, consuming only one night at a time. I was to make sure the rotating beacon was indeed rotating, check that the transient maintenance guys were awake, ensure that the airfield lights were lit, greet arriving VIPs, (I once welcomed astronaut John Young to Nellis) and handle anything unusual. The guys and gals who really ran the "aerodrome" knew their jobs well and needed little help from junior captains. I got the impression that my role was to take control if things got out of hand and to adsorb the blame if anything went amiss.

On my first night as the AO, I reported to Base Operations to get my tasking. The Lt. Col. running Base Operations gave me a 20-minute briefing and handed me a 50-page loose-leaf notebook covering the duties of the AO. Half of the briefing and half of the notebook were concerned, very concerned indeed, with preventing Mr. Hughes from landing at Nellis Air Force Base, Nevada.

Exactly a year earlier, at 0200 hours, Mr. Hughes left his well-guarded digs on the 13th floor of the Desert Inn Hotel and Casino on the Vegas strip. He departed in a blacked-out ambulance convoyed by his all-Mormon staff in other vehicles. Vegas being Vegas, word of Hughes' movement spread like the desert winds. Most major news outlets had spies on retainer in the Desert Inn to alert the newshounds if Mr. Hughes ever left the 13th floor. Howard Hughes was the biggest story in Vegas. He owned about half the Las Vegas Strip. Quickly his motorcade was intercepted and chased by a squadron of paparazzi, reporters, and TV news teams. The ambulance, its escorts, and numerous pursuers drove northeast, out through North Las Vegas, to the main gate at Nellis. As a military contractor through the Hughes Aircraft Company, Mr. Hughes was entitled to enter the base. His vehicles all had base access stickers on their windshields. The newshounds did not and were firmly stopped by the gate guard, leaving them outside and blinding them to what Hughes was up to. An executive jet landed at Nellis and picked up the reclusive Hughes, then disappeared into the night, its owner unsighted by the reporters. The AO on duty that night had passively watched this momentous event unfold without notifying any senior officer, which turned out to be definitely a career-limiting omission. Once the business jet took off, the AO went back to bed.

At 0700 the next morning, the Major General who ran Nellis received a call from Hank Greenspun, the outspoken, larger-than-life publisher of the Las Vegas Review-Journal, Sin City's major newspaper. Greenspun was a Vegas legend himself, having moved out to Nevada from Chicago to run his own news rag. He was rumored to have been in tight with that much-beloved Vegas civic planner, Bugsy Siegel. On the phone, the newspaperman chewed out the general for not allowing the press to cover the biggest story of the year in Vegas, the departure of Howard Hughes. If there's anything that generals love, it's surprises. They enjoy even more getting lectured on the freedom of the press by civilian media hacks, the ink-stained wretches of the fourth estate, with supposed gang land connections.

Orders were issued. Howard Hughes was forever barred from Nellis no matter how many contracts Hughes Aircraft was awarded. The hapless AO that night was probably transferred to run the motor pool at Lonely AFB, Alaska. This unfortunate episode generated the set of detailed instructions I received at Base Ops. If I got word of any impending landing by Howard Hughes, I was to turn out the airfield lights, shut down the airport, block the runways with the base fire trucks, call out the Air Police, and wake up the Commanding General., not necessarily in that order.

After ensuring that the rotating beacon was indeed rotating, I ate dinner at the Officers' Club, with no booze, and checked into the Visiting Officers Quarters. Before turning in, I switched on local TV's late news show. The lead story screamed, "Billionaire Howard Hughes Has Left the Park Lane Hotel in London, Destination Unknown." Holy Shit! I carefully re-read the instruction book and, with nothing else to be done at the time, went to bed.

At 0100, the phone rang. It was the sergeant manning the control tower.

"Captain Cobleigh?"

I answered, "Yo."

He went on, "Sir, an unauthorized civilian aircraft has just landed on the inner runway." Oh No! I asked, "What have you done?"

The reply came back, "We've secured the aircraft. The Air Police have the occupants spread-eagled on the ramp."

Panicked, I blurted out, "Is it Howard Hughes?"

The enlisted air traffic controller, knowing full well that Hughes hadn't been seen in public for decades, replied, "I don't know, Sir. What does Howard Hughes look like?"

Just great! My career was going down in flames and I had Bob Hope staffing the tower.

I leaped out of bed and into my USAF-issued pick-up truck, turned on the blue bubble gum machine light on the roof, and zorched down to the flight line. Getting nearer, I could see a white civilian aircraft dimly outlined on the tarmac by the red flashing lights of the security vehicles. I skidded to a stop in the dirt beside the pavement and walked slowly up to the scene, trying hard to be cool, I saw three prone figures lying face down on the tarmac with M-16's pointed at their backs. I thought, *If one of those guys is tall and wearing a snap-brim fedora with a leather flying jacket, I'm going to turn around, drive out the main gate, and leave my wings and commission with the gate guard.*

The intruders proved to be three scared guys in a Beechcraft Bonanza who had mistaken Nellis for the civilian field, North Las Vegas Air Terminal. My instructions on accidental civilian use by pilots other than Howard Hughes were clear. I was to verify their pilot licenses, flight physicals, insurance, flight plans, aircraft records, yada, yada, yada. I did none of that. I ordered the Air Police to let the guys up. Much relieved, I told the shaken civilians;

"North Las Vegas Air Terminal is 350 degrees for 10 nm. Get back in your bug smasher, take off, and never come back here."

As things were wrapping up, I called Johnny Carson up in the tower, "Chief, did you notify the General?"

He replied, "No Sir, that's your job."

I told him, "Then, let's let this be our little secret, shall we?"

That's the night I (almost) met Howard Hughes. Mr. Hughes eventually landed in Nicaragua, wherever that is.

CHAPTER FIFTEEN
WESTERN IRAN. 1973/74

Iran, It Wasn't How You Think

Late at night, the gently rolling plains of Western Iran were haunted by ghostly images not seen, their presence only felt. That's how they appeared to me. Or did I imagine them to be there? Under a moonless sky, the inverted bowl of blinking stars was stirred by a dry wind. The wind-blown desert dust seemed to move the blue-white dots across the *noir* sky. The night was pitch black, lightened only by the moving sand. The two-lane highway remained un-lit except for the feeble headlights of our car peering into the swirling dust clouds blown across the road by the stiff breeze.

Five of us were returning from dinner in Hamadan, Iran, a desert town, the regional capital, with a legitimate claim to be the oldest continually inhabited city on earth. It looked the part with layers upon layers of ancient and half-forgotten civilizations built on top of one another. The Persian meal we enjoyed at a local restaurant was unfamiliar but excellent.

In the front seat driving was one of my squadron mates, Siead, a fighter pilot with the Imperial Iranian Air Force, IIAF, and his wife, Myna. A surprise addition to the dinner party was Siead's sister-in-law, a young, raven-haired Persian woman, a pretty nurse with excellent command of English. She, and another American FWS IP, Captain Tom Hood, were with me in the back seat.

As I watched the dusty wind-swept landscape pass slowly by, I remembered how these contoured plains had been crossed by countless invaders, by many tramping armies through the eons of time. Alexander the Great of Greece, Darius the Great of old Persia, (evidently "The Great" was a popular handle back then) the Golden Mongol Horde, the Turks, the British Army, all marched across these lands, eastward and westward, enroute to conquest, plunder, glory, and sometimes disaster.

99

Their ghostly ranks were out there in the night. I couldn't see them, but I could sense their presence, while they were bearing the weight of history.

The Persian cutie, watching me peer out the closed car window, asked, "Captain Ed. what are you looking for?" She slowly put her hand on my knee and wrapped her fingers between my legs. While this gesture was unexpected, it did not come as a complete surprise. In Iran, female nurses didn't have the purest of reputations, similar to those of truck stop waitresses in the USA, due to their daily interactions with males they weren't married to. The religious/tribal elders ruled that healing the sick was incompatible with chastity. The Mullahs preemptively proscribed these women as prostitutes for having the audacity to A) seek a profession outside the home and B) deal independently with men. Despite this imposed injustice I felt compelled to reply with a neutral response.

"Ghosts. They're there, I know it." I let her hand stay where it was. I didn't think that was the answer she was looking for.

The juxtaposition between the two images, one ethereal and external, and one very real next to me, was jarring. During my stays in Iran, I came to understand how the role and place of women in the local Persian society had been, and still was, constrained by omnipresent Muslim/tribal dogma. A millennia-and-a-half ago, the first mullahs incorporated their rigid desert tribal restrictions on females into their emerging religion. Those forces of gender oppression were represented by the ghostly armies of ignorance parading out there in the night. Inside the modern car, a Persian woman, a Muslim, offered me an obvious invitation, breaking many centuries of taboo. She was Iran's future. Its past was out there in the darkness and backwardness.

Why was I there, in the Iranian hinterland, crossing the night in a beat-up Peykan, Farsi for "Arrow," a Toyota built under license in Iran, bouncing along a straight, almost deserted highway? It was a long distance from Las Vegas in more ways than one. The story starts with the Shah of Iran.

In the 1970s, the Shah got whatever he wanted, whenever he asked, from Uncle Sam. His official title was His Imperial Majesty the Shahenshah, the king of kings. Americans stationed in Iran as members of the US military liaison team mission referred to him as" Fred" among themselves to avoid accidently offending their Persian hosts by omitting the required verbal protocols if they were overheard talking about the Shah

The Shah was intent on making Iran into a regional power using the country's stupendous oil revenues. He also leveraged the western powers' desire to maintain some political order in a tough, oil-rich neighborhood. Iran was a good customer for advanced American weaponry. The Persians paid cash, on time, and didn't demand industrial offsets or local production. Along with the hardware came US military advisors and trainers, that would be me. We all reported to a USAF two-star, General Dan Duren, at the US Embassy in Teheran, the capital. The Imperial Iranian Air Force Commander, General Katahami, wanted instructors from the Fighter Weapons School to help train his rapidly expanding air force. IPs from the FWS were dispatched every summer to embed with Persian squadrons in Iran. My Ops Officer at Nellis told me "Tag, you're it" for two summer tours.

I was surprised to go as it meant flying and training with the Persians at a remote base way west of Teheran. But I was curious to see what Iran was like after knowing three Persian student pilots in UPT. One summer Tom Hood and I trained pilots on how to fly Phantom's latest version, the F-4E LES. This modification installed leading edge slats, LES, on the wings curing many of the aircraft's handling vices. Another year, Phil Comstock, Mike VanWagenen, and I instructed in the operation of the AGM-65 Maverick TV-guided missile. We arrived in-country with no formal syllabus, no visual aids, no lessons ready, no proscribed number of flights, and no plan. We were told to pick up F-4s from Mehrabad AFB in Teheran, fly them to Shahrokhi AFB and do what we needed to do, making it up on the fly, literally. Fortunately, we all had instructed in the transition to the LES Phantoms and in Maverick employment at Nellis. All we had to do was to adapt our operations to the Persians' somewhat limited skill set.

Disembarking from the Trans World Airlines Boeing 707 and taking a taxi into central Teheran the first time was an eye-opening revelation. This was my only visit to a city in that part of the world. The burg was booming. Teheran sprawls at the base of a mountain range which separates the dry southern plains from the Caspian Sea to the north. The northern suburbs were prosperous, with walled villas, jaguar sedans, fancy restaurants, and western garb. The further south in Teheran you went, the further back in time you traveled until you reached the bazaar, a labyrinth of hawkers' shops straight out of the Middle Ages, only with electricity.

Teheran's streets were crowded and chaotic. Traffic rules were advisory only. It wasn't uncommon to have a taxi driver cross over the double yellow line to pass or to take to the sidewalk to avoid a snarl. Most Persians were friendly to Americans, many wanted to practice their English. One young lady asked me if I was a representative of "Shah Nixon." It seemed that some folks were emerging into the modern world while others were mired in a reactionary Muslim past, depending on which part of Teheran you were in.

The sidewalks were awash in women wearing the traditional *Chador*, an all-black flowing robe which left only their faces uncovered. Mixed in with the "black moving objects" were younger women, some in all-black, skin-tight cat suits and others sporting the latest Parisian fashions. Persian women are, on average, the best looking in the world. It was jarring to see such a wide range of female dress, some religiously imposed and some overtly sensuous.

Of course, the Iranian men were under no obligation for any sort of religious dress rules. Or mixed gender behavior rules for that matter. Many men had yet to grasp the requirements of polite life in the 20th century. One of the embassy official's wives told me when she went out, wearing normal clothes like jeans, she always carried a rolled-up magazine to swat away groping hands.

Every major street in Teheran was bounded on each side by a topless, concrete-lined ditch, an open sanitary drain. Checking into our hotel for the first night, I couldn't help but think, *What these people need is not a missile system but a sewer system.*

One aspect of life in Teheran was, and remains, a mystery to me to this day. A popular family destination and a favorite hang-out for teenagers was a large ice cream shop. Capacity was in the hundreds with folks slurping excellent ice cream and tasty frozen yogurt. The name of the place was "Chattanooga," even spelled correctly. I never found out why my hometown provided its moniker for a much larger Persian version of Baskin Robbins. After an in-brief at the Embassy and some more great ice cream, we flew to our duty station, checking in with our IIAF squadron mates.

The airbase was still under construction, or being upgraded, and the quarters for the married junior officers weren't yet finished. So, most of the guys we flew with, and their wives, lived with us in the Bachelor

Officers Quarters, the BOQ. Persian social customs took some getting used to for uncouth fighter pilots from Sin City. The pilots were a social lot, with numerous parties and communal meals at the Officers Club. I would be talking to a squadron mate who would have his wife by his side. He would make no effort to introduce her or even give me her name. The woman would not acknowledge my presence on the planet, looking straight ahead, not at me, saying not a word.

Our immediate contact at the US Embassy was Major Jim LeFleur, a F-4 pilot himself. After a few days, he came out to fly with us. I asked him what was the deal with the Persian wives. Jim told me all Persians believed that American fighter pilots were hot to bed any woman they could get their hands on. At the time, there was some truth to that. Under the strict Muslim rules of female conduct, any contact at all with a sex-crazed American would besmirch the woman's precious honor forever. Jim counseled us to go easy on social interactions. Once the Persians saw that we were straight arrows, they would open up. That is exactly what happened. Eventually we developed warm friendships with the wives as well as their husbands.

Another quirk of Persian behavior prompted another question for LeFleur. We were invited to dinner at the house of the one-star general who ran the base. All the top brass were there with their fashionably-dressed wives. It was an elegant evening with a multi-course, candlelight dinner. Persian senior officers knew how to live. The long table was set with Waterford crystal, Spode china, and sterling silver flatware. That is except for us Americans. Our place settings included plain white ceramic plates, ordinary wine glasses, and steel flatware from the Officers Club bin. That slight didn't prevent us from having a good meal and a great time. LeFleur later explained the set-up. We Americans were infidels, non-believers in Islam. After the meal, all the things we has touched were destroyed so no senior Muslim would ever have to share a plate or a glass with a heathen. This fastidiousness didn't extend to the O Club itself, where junior officers and Americans shared and shared alike. Also, the Koran's prohibition on the consumption of alcohol didn't seem to apply anywhere we ate, and drank.

On one training mission, Jim was in my back seat. The IIAF ground crew was young and motivated as we started the F-4. Once the pre-flight checks were complete, I motioned to the Crew Chief to pull the wheel chocks. As we taxied out, he flashed a snappy hand salute. I returned the gesture with my best Tom Cruise shit-eating-grin and a "thumbs up" straight out of the movie *Top Gun*. Instead of a smile, the enlisted man frowned and turned away.

I asked LeFleur over the inter-cockpit intercom, "What's up with the Crew Chief? He seems pissed."

Jim came back, "That's because you just gave him the finger."

Evidently, different fingers mean different things in different cultures. After the flight, we found the offended guy and with the help of a pilot/interpreter, I apologized and explained. I guessed he never saw the movie. The poor guy was dumbfounded. In the rigidly hierarchical IIAF, it was unthinkable for an officer to apologize to an enlisted troop for anything. Afterward, Jim and I shared a bottle of wine at the O Club, de-briefing social *faux pas*.

Iran produced some quite reasonable red wine, which the Persians called "Shiraz." This is the Australian term for the French Syrah grape. How a French/Aussie grape got to Iran is beyond me, but I was glad it did. However, most guys we dealt with, young and old alike, drank vodka, which they pronounced "wodka," mixed with lime juice over ice. If there was any religious prohibition against alcohol consumption, it got checked at the O Club's front door.

The food at the club, and in town, was tasty and healthful. A typical meal would include skewers of grilled meat, lamb, beef, or occasionally chicken, never pork, and a mound of Persian rice. The rice was crispy and quite a production to make. Persian rice is like Texas bar-b-que, every cook has his/her own recipe and technique which they consider to be superior to all others. Super-fresh flat bread accompanied each meal. An unsweetened yogurt drink washed things down. Dessert tended to be fruit, particularly sweet Persian melons, somewhat like a green cantaloupe. Not bad chow for an O Club in the middle of nowhere.

Once we got in tight with the guys and their wives, I learned a lot about Iran, its people, and their dreams for their country. With sworn enemies all around, the Persians I got to know were dedicated on making Iran a modern powerhouse, the Germany of the middle east. Indeed, they counted Germany as a role model, even calling themselves "Aryans." Persians are not Arabs, to call one an Arab is a grave insult. They are not Turks whom they also look down on. Nor are they Pakistanis who they consider to be weird. Referring to themselves as Aryans was a way to establish an emotional link with Germany regardless of the lack of genetic or historical connections. Most Persians were dark-complected with black hair and ebony eyes, not your typical blond-haired, blue-eyed

Aryans, but what the heck. The Persians did have one tenuous connection with Germans. Both cultures seem to believe that the letters "W" and "V" are interchangeable. Hence in the Rhineland you'll hear, "I vant to see the wineyards" and hear "wodka" in Iran. While a "W" is merely a double "V" and English is basically French spoken by Germans, the mix-up of the two letters is strange wherever it occurs.

One thing my squadron mates agreed on is the need for Iran to develop its own atomic weapons. There was no debate on this point. Nukes would be their entry into the top tier of nations. I believe this goal is still on the national schedule.

All the IIAF officers spoke passable English as did many young men I encountered. Among the Persian elite fluency in English was a ticket to success. For the guys that is, for some reason, many women studied French instead of English. I told one wife that, in America, we called French the language of love. She replied that English must be the language of war as whenever there was armed conflict, one side usually spoke English. Ouch!

Over two summers, I came to respect the Persians and their plans for the future of their country. Sadly, all my contacts were with the elite, the English and French speakers, the folks who lived in the northern suburbs of Teheran. I never met nor got to know the rural folks who lived in traditional ways and who were fervent Muslims. Fred the Shah's plan to modernized Iran excluded them as well as the religious social infrastructure and its mullahs. This alienation and exclusion eventually fermented into the Iranian revolution which put paid to the Shah and his minions. The Persian elite either fled the country or hunkered down. I believe there still to be enlightened people in Iran, people who chafe under the fundamentalist theoracary's corrupt, yet fanatical rule and would like to regain again the dream of a modern, prosperous Iran.

We did have some limited contact with rural folks. The BOQ building was maintained and cleaned by two young men in their late teens. They were enlisted members of the IIAF. Using our squadron mates as interpreters, we learned their story. Their official title translated as "available heads." Their heads were available for use and for sacrifice by the state. The IIAF issued our Maverick training team a set of wheels, a Land Rover right out of Daktari with the spare tire mounted flat on the hood. We called it the "Maverick Mobile." With our help, the two orderlies learned to drive it.

The pair came from a remote farm village in northeast Iran. One night the Iranian army encircled the village and come the dawn, our two guys found themselves in the military. Claiming to have bone spurs on their heels wouldn't have gotten them a deferment from the heavily-armed draft board. They did view their service with some fondness. Through it, they learned a marketable skill they could use when they returned home, the ability to drive a car/truck. At the time, I viewed these two flunky-butts as symbolic of the future of rural Iran. I wonder what happened to them after the Iranian counter-revolution of 1979 catapulted the country back into the Dark Ages.

Social progress or no, our job in Iran was to train and fly. That was the best part.

CHAPTER SIXTEEN
SHAHROKHI AFB, IRAN

Killing the Shah, Almost

By the mid-1970s, USAF F-4 Phantoms were tired, many were worn out. Years of combat missions in Vietnam coupled with intensive training missions in the US all had taken their toll. At Nellis, we flew the newest F-4Es in the fleet but even there the aircraft were often unavailable awaiting repairs or spare parts. As the SEA conflict wound down the constant protests against that sorry-ass war and against the US military in general also affected our USAF personnel. Morale, particularly among the enlisted troops, measured lower than whale poop. Spare parts were hard to come by. Trained maintainers left the service in droves for greener and less controversial pastures. It was not uncommon to plan for flight of four F-4s at 0600 and find out after the pre-mission briefing there were only enough serviceable aircraft for a flight of two, or a flight of none. At least we got briefing practice.

Flying with the IIAF in Iran was like being in a brand-new air force. The jets were pristine, right from the factory, and well-maintained by enthusiastic troops. Everything on the air base was shiny new, no expense had been spared. There was even a bakery on base furnishing fresh "nan" bread for every meal. The bakery was run by a guy who reminded me of scroungy Cookie, the mess sergeant, in the Beatle Baily comic strip, but his product was yummy.

The Persian pilots were eager to fly and eager to learn. They tended to fall into two camps. The first, smaller group was comprised of old heads. These guys had logged thousands of hours of flying time, trained in the US in fighters, and knew what they were doing in the air. Two of these pilots were among the best aircraft handlers I ever flew with. They could get it done. These two went on to command the first two F-14 Tomcat squadrons when the Shah bought that heavy-metal advanced fighter to replace his brand-new F-4s. The second, and larger, group were

107

guys recently out of UPT who had upgraded to the F-4 in Iran. What they lacked in experience, they made up for in enthusiasm.

Having no combat experience and no advanced in-country training, the IIAF pilots' tactical knowledge was rudimentary at best. Both summers I was there, our USAF teams tried to instill some ideas about how combat operations should be conducted in addition to the curriculum we were being paid to teach. It was a tight group, flying together and living together in the BOQ.

The training kicked off with academic classroom presentations. With USAF students, I always began my lectures by telling a joke to lighten things up. I didn't know how my American sense of humor would go over in Iran. So, I got the guys to tell me what the Persians found amusing. I also got someone to write in Farsi, "My name is Ed Cobleigh, welcome to Maverick class." The first day, my verbal joke and my inscription, written on a white board, got lots of yuks. After class, the guys told me they weren't laughing at my lame joke but at my handwriting. Farsi is written right-to-left. I wrote my memorized greeting left-to-right, backwards.

One day, I mentioned to the IIAF Squadron Commander that I enjoyed undergraduate pilot training with Jalal Payami. I asked if he knew him. The next day, "Black Camel" showed up at the base on a day out-and-back flight in his F-5A Freedom Fighter after a phone call from the squadron CO. Payami served in a F-5 squadron piloting the lightweight fighter Northrop built and sold for international sales. He was also a member of the IIAF aerial demonstration team in the F-5 putting on airshows like the USAF Thunderbirds and the USN Blue Angels. It was sure good to see him, to catch up, and to relive UPT stories.

When Maverick training was complete, the Base Commander wanted to put on a demonstration of these wonder-missiles from the future, or from the USA. A successful firepower demo would enhance his cred with the top brass. While we were helping organize the airshow, we learned the Commander of the IIAF and the Shah of Iran, Fred himself, would attend. No pressure there.

The enlisted crew turned to and parked two junked trucks side-by-side on the far side of the runway, past a hurriedly-built reviewing stand on the near side. They painted the wrecks black for good contrast with the desert sand. A nearby hill was painted with a semi-circle of black to simulate a cave/tunnel entrance. Set in front of the fake cave were barrels of a mixture of diesel and jet fuel, all the better to produce an explosion signifying a direct hit. These were easy Maverick targets.

On the big day, I waited in the O Club for the VIPs to arrive. Mike VanWagenen would brief the flight at the squadron, and Phil Comstock would fly in the shooter's back seat. Delivering the ordnance would be Major Vieasy, the squadron Ops Officer and a recent graduate of our Maverick school.

The first VIP to arrive was the Commander of the IIAF, General Khatami. If you called over to Central Casting and requested a Chief of the Air Force, that was the guy you would get. Six foot two, broad shoulders, alethic build, smooth stride, silver/black hair close cropped, hawk's nose, firm handshake. The general looked you directly in the eye when he talked. While we were waiting, we sipped tea at the O Club. The Commander thanked me and the team for spending time in Iran away from our families and for training his pilots. I assured him we thoroughly enjoyed the experience of working with his dedicated men. That got a smile from the Boss.

In time, the Shah arrived and all the officers present at the club, including me, stood in a receiving line, saluting as His Imperial Majesty, Mohammed Reza Pahlavi walked by. Actually, "walked" is the wrong term. "teetered" or "stumbled" would be more accurate. It took exactly one look to sum up Fred. The Shah was a small man, five-two or five-three, and very concerned about his height or rather his lack thereof. He wore the immaculately-tailored IIAF uniform of a senior general or field marshal, festooned with numerous ribbons, medals, and badges. I never found out what all those "gongs" were for but I'll bet they weren't awarded for participation in aerial flight.

That would be the King of Jordan, an accomplished pilot, who flew the F-104 Starfighter in the Royal Jordanian Air Force and probably not as a wingman. It's good to be King. But I digress. The Shah wore zip-up black boots with half-inch soles and two-inch heels. There were also lifts inside his boots as well, from the look of them. The pair of elevator shoes added a couple of inches in much-desired height but made the Shah of Iran walk like Brazilian singer Carmen Miranda on her platform shoes, only without the fruit salad hat. The colorful "fruit salad" was the ribbons on his diminutive chest. The Shah exhibited a Napoleon complex but without the Little General's genius for leadership and organization.

Then, it was show time. The worthies, including strangely enough, me, were assembled on the reviewing stand on the ramp next to the runway. General Khatami stood next to the Shah. I stood nervously 15 or 20 feet to their right, even with the pair, as no one was allowed to stand behind the Shah.

The occupant of the Peacock Throne, I am not making that up, was very concerned about assignation. His father was politically murdered and the Shah himself survived at least three attempts on his own life. He traveled with a troop of bodyguards, his version of the US Secret Service. This special forces unit was called "The Immortals," the same title as the praetorian guard dedicated to the protection of King Darius the Great of old-time Persia. That unit name wasn't a coincidence. A squad of Immortals lined the rear of the reviewing stand, fully armed and ready to take a bullet for the Shah. Beside me was an IIAF one-star general with a mike cord leading down to a Forward Air Control, FAC, Jeep which was in radio contact with the demo aircraft.

The shooter F-4 approached from right-to-left parallel to the far side of the runway. Phil Comstock in the rear cockpit locked the Maverick's TV seeker onto the target trucks. Then things went wildly off the rails, literally.

The Maverick's black-and-white TV seeker requires the target be a minimum size or else the electronic lock-on will not survive the violent transients experienced during launch from the aircraft. The jet-black trucks against the light desert allowed Phil to lock on way early, out of range. Major Vieasy should have waited until the target grew in size on the cockpit displays. But he acquired a bad case of buck fever and pushed the pickle button too soon. The missile came off the launcher rail, rocket motor firing, and promptly broke lock with the target. When a Maverick breaks lock, it always performs a climbing turn to the left, a chandelle in aerobatic terms. The second act of the screw-up was much worse than the first.

The prime directive of all air show ordinance delivery procedures is; DON'T RELEASE MUNITIONS UNTIL PAST THE REVIEWING STAND, PARTICULARLY WITH FORWARD-FIRING DEVICES LIKE GUIDED MISSILES! Or in this case, an un-guided missile. I saw the rocket motor ignite well before passing where we were standing and knew instantly what was about to happen. The Maverick cleared the aircraft and turned left, headed directly at the reviewing stand, pointed at us. I did not take this as a positive development.

I thought if I survived the missile's impact, the Immortals would surely kill me as the whole scenario looked exactly like an attempt to wipe out the Shah with a missile attack launched by a rogue IIAF fighter pilot. Fortunately, the Maverick continued its gentle chandelle climb and passed directly over the reviewing stand at about 1000 feet of altitude. It headed south, out in the desert, never to be seen again. Deep breath on my part.

I got on the radio and told Phil to make another run, there were three missiles on the F-4, and for God's sake, don't let Vieasy pickle off the bird until the target loomed large in the cockpit scope and the aircraft passed the crowd. This transmission was completely un-necessary, except for the requested re-attack, as Phil already knew what went wrong. The Phantom circled the air field and made another pass. This time, the Maverick guided true and blew the trucks to smithereens, whatever they are.

The cave attack was next on the playbill. Same flight profile, past the reviewing stand, whew, only the target was on a distant hill. The missile launched. The rocket motor burned for the proscribed five seconds. Then the smoke trail petered out. The missile climbed for more range and was instantly lost to sight from the ground. The predicated flight duration computed to be about 45 seconds, an eternity in air show time. My bad, I neglected to inform the viewers as to what they were about to see.

Once the missile disappeared the Shah and the top General waited a few seconds, maybe ten, and then assumed another miss. The Shah turned and shook hands with the Commander. One of three direct hits isn't too bad, he seemed to say. You couldn't do that with dumb bombs. As the Shah started to walk away, the fake cave erupted in a bright-red explosion then spurted a volcano of fire and smoke. What a show! The Shah turned back, shook hands again, a grin on his small face, and left for Teheran. I left to meet Phil and Mike at the O club bar.

A few days later, four of us went into town for another excellent dinner. On the way back, as we were driving around a traffic circle, or roundabout as the Brits say, we heard a loud "Crump" and saw a cloud of dust spurt from a construction site nearby. A bricklayer's scaffold had collapsed. We jumped from the car and ran to the scene. Lying face down among a pile of bricks was a body. I instantly wished I had paid better attention during buddy-care first-aid class. The accident victim was a young man, in his late teens or early twenties. After a quick exam, we saw he had a bloody broken nose, a broken collar bone, and a possibly broken arm from doing a face plant from the falling scaffold. We bundle the guy into the car and drove him to the local Persian hospital's version of an Emergency Room.

There the ER doctor did a quick exam of his own and then quoted to our two IIAF pilots a projected fee, cash on the barrel head, for treatment. The message was clear, no money, no treatment. We pooled all our available cash. The sum fell short. After a negotiation, every price in Iran is negotiable, the Doc accepted all our money, bills and coins, and led the youth away. As we were leaving the hospital, an older man came running up. He was the head of the construction company and the injured guy's father. Pulling out a stuffed wallet, he repaid us for our expenditures. With tears in his eyes, he thanked us profusely for caring for his injured son. During the drive back to the base, Saied, who was driving, said, "My God will thank me for that." Indeed.

Maverick and LES training complete, the team returned to Teheran for out-briefing with the Embassy and with General <u>Dan</u> Duren and some serious partying.

Chapter Seventeen
Done in Teheran

Leaving Louisiana, or Iran, in the Broad Daylight

It's easy to poke fun at a strutting popinjay such as the ex-Shah of Iran. However, we should cut the little guy some slack. The Shah and his twin sister, Ashray Pahlavi, who many believed to be the brains behind the Peacock Throne, tried their best to build Iran into a modern, prosperous country. Princess Ashray particularly focused on liberating women from some of their traditional Islamic shackles. She believed women should be treated like human beings instead of chattel. Of course, rapid economic growth enriched the Pahlavi family and their elite, foreign-educated friends in Teheran, enraging the country's many have-nots. Push-back was the result. The reactionary forces were made up of the clergy, the mullahs, and the ayatollahs teamed with *bourgeoise,* the merchants in the bazar. Together they toppled the Shah and his sister in 1979, establishing a Muslim theocracy throughout Iran. The primitive religious establishment resented their loss of moral/legal authority over society and hated uppity womenfolk who refused to wear veils or even headscarves. The other half of the conspiracy, the bazar community, possessed neither the means nor the skillset to cash in on the economic boom. Their beef with the Pahlavis was mainly financial. They wanted a slice of the ever-growing pie.

Fred should have read his Persian history books more carefully. Darius The Great abandoned his Immortals during a losing battle and fled the scene in a chariot. They then turned on him. When the revolutionary mobs to the teeming streets in Teheran, the Shah's own Immortals melted away, discarding their uniforms. The Shah and his sister left Teheran by private jet never to return.

Despite his forward social thinking, the Shah exhibited many authoritarian impulses. He was no little "D" democrat. He also possessed the means to impose his rule. I learned this the hard way. At a large outdoor reception in Hamadan, I was thunder-struck by one of the most beautiful women I have ever seen. She resembled a young Elizabeth Taylor, only prettier with a better figure. Her bight green silk dress displayed her every curve in excruciating detail. She had attended the party with her husband, an older man. He projected a perpetual stern look, a scowl on his face, and rigid mannerisms. Obviously not a guy to trifle with.

Standing with a group of IIAF pilots, I asked one to introduce me to the woman in the green dress. I wanted nothing more than to say I spoke to this world-class, raven-haired beauty. Instantly, the guys started looking down at their shuffling feet or up at the night sky. One left quickly to refresh his drink. Finally, one mumbled, "No can do, Captain Ed." I dropped the subject like a dumb bomb. There was more going on with the beauteous babe than the normal Muslim female honor system coupled with an over-protective husband.

When the party ended, I passed the woman on the way out. I smiled at her. She smiled at me.

I said, "Je pense que vous êtes très belle." I think you are very beautiful.

She replied, "Merci beaucoup. Vous êtes très gentil, Monsieur Americain." Thank you. You are very kind, Mr. American.

A few days later, the truth came out. The Persian woman was the wife of the local head of SAVAK, the Shah's secret police. Yikes! Everyone at the party knew who he was but me. Leaving aside how well-known the commander of the "secret" police was, it was common knowledge that to cross him would earn a miscreant a cell in the notorious Evin prison in Teheran.

I was glad that when I spoke to her, I used the formal French state of address, the "vous" form intended for strangers. Had I used the familiar "tu" form, used when speaking to wives and/or lovers, I probably would have been whacked by SAVAK.

Once on the US TV show, "60 Minutes," the reporter asked the Shah about reports there were 250 SAVAK agents in the US gathering information. The Shah replied he hoped so, that's what he paid them to do. Politically correct Fred was not.

One of our last nights in Teheran, the IIAF pilots laid on a going away party at a local outdoor night club. Most of the guys and their wives were there. Despite Jalal Payami's protestation that he never saw a camel in Iran, much less driven one, Persian restaurants tended to imitate a desert oasis. Open air, under the stars, lit by strings of naked light bulbs, in the center bubbled a fountain in a small pool. Radiating from the pool like spokes of a wheel were tiny streams in concrete runs. Along the flowing brooks were scattered communal wooden tables. It was a charming scene with excellent Persian food and drinks. After dinner, the guys participated in what seemed to me to be a poetry recitation. Each stood in turn and recited a short piece with much emotion displayed. My Farsi is weak to non-existent so I didn't understand a word, but I got the impression of series of sad poems. It was a contest, with fighter pilots what else could it have been? As the progression got around to where I sat, the other American beside me asked, "What are we going to do?"

I replied, "Not to worry. I've got this."

When it came around the table to be my turn, one of the guys told me, "You don't have to compete, Captain Ed."

Now I couldn't back down. I stood up and began a tragic, epic poem I learned as a boy:

> *The outlook wasn't brilliant for the Mudville nine that day,*
> *The score stood four to two with but one inning left to play,*
>
> *They thought, "If only Casey could but get a whack at that,"*
> *They put up even money now with Casey at the bat,*

The guys understood the words. Some wives could as well, but no one knew diddly about baseball. As I went on, I laid it on thicker and deeper, waving my hands with animation, my face showing raw emotion:

> *Close by the sturdy batsman the ball unheeded sped,*
> *"That ain't my style," said Casey. "Strike one," the umpire said.*

I put on my sad face, lowered my voice, gazed around with downcast eyes and wrapped it up:

> *Oh, somewhere in this favored land the sun is shining bright,*
> *The band is playing somewhere, and somewhere hearts are light;*

And somewhere men are laughing, and somewhere children shout,
But there is no joy in Mudville—mighty Casey has struck out.

I won a bottle of "wodka" which I contributed to the party on the spot. We left Iran the next morning. I enjoyed my two assignments in Iran but it was always good to leave. I missed my wife and daughter. After experiencing the exotic and ancient cities of old Persia, I was ready to get back to that good ole typical American home town, Las Vegas, Nevada.

Sometimes it is OK to be in the right place at the wrong time. During our out-briefing with General Duren, I expected to be reamed a new one over the goat-rope of an airshow we staged. However, the general was gracious. He thanked us for our service and sent us on our way with no mention of trying to kill the Shah of Iran. I know if I helped organize a firepower demo which shot a live missile over the heads of the Chief of Staff of the United States Air Force and the President of the USA, my next duty assignment would have been an un-accompanied tour as the gooney bird (albatross) control officer at Wake Island AFB.

I did regret that there was no way to pass on the corporate knowledge to follow-on training teams in Iran. One good example was the correct way to de-brief an IIAF training flight. For instance, picture a sortie designed to demonstrate the improved handling of the LES F-4s. At 30,000 feet, the student would be called upon to reduce the engine power to idle and let the airspeed decay through 150 knots, about 175 mph, then roll the aircraft with the ailerons through the control stick, coordinating the roll with rudder inputs. This just like in a normal aircraft, requiring the student to un-learn the un-natural roll the jet with rudder and keep the stick centered as on the "hard wing" Phantoms.

If the lesson didn't go well, back on the ground, I would have debriefed an American pilot as follows:

"Well, Ace, that was moderately screwed up. Let's review what you did wrong and how you can learn to do it the right way."

If I used the same terminology and approach with a Persian pilot, I would have gotten back one or more of the following excuses: 1. "Language problem, I didn't understand the instructions." 2. "Flight control malfunction." 3. "The sun got in my eyes." 4. "The dog ate my homework."

With the Persians, you had to take the following tack: "Mohammed, that maneuver did not go as we wanted and it's all my fault. I'm sorry. If

I was a better IP, I could have taught you how to succeed. Let me see if I can do better on the next flight tomorrow."

When I debased myself as an IP, inevitably the student would come back with:

"No, no, Captain Ed, I messed that up. I'll do it right next time."

It's a pity that all the effort, time and attention we spent in Iran has been swept away

By the so-called "Revolution." Aren't revolutions supposed to bring in the future, not the past? Maybe someday, the proud Persian people will have had enough, will rise up, and reclaim their dreams and their heritage from the corrupt, backward ayatollahs who are running the proud country of Iran into the desert sands.

After the revolution, a few pilots we trained stayed on in the air force, growing proper Islamic beards under their oxygen masks. Intel sources reported that during the Iran-versus-Iraq war, an invasion of Iran by the Iraqi army was blunted by close air support. In one battle, a flight of four F-4s firing Mavericks logged 11 armored vehicles destroyed out of 12 missiles launched. There was no way to confirm or disprove the covert report but the claimed kill rate tracks with historical Maverick combat data. Another F-4 pilot, call sign "Maverick" of all handles, made a name for himself punching holes in the sides of Iraqi tankers with his namesake missile.

You would think a missile designed to take out tanks and armored vehicles would generate conflagrations when deployed against oil tankers. You would be wrong. First, tankers are not easy targets. The TV tracker in the missile's seeker is optimized for pinpoint targets, not immense ships. For esoteric electronic reasons, when launched against a ship the missile tends to fly over it, much like one did above the Shah and me. The Taiwan Chinese air force once put on a Maverick demo missing an entire island. Second, tankers are not as flammable as you would think. Exhaust gas from the diesel engines is piped into the air space over the liquid in the hull's tanks. There is not enough oxygen in the head space to ignite the crude oil. A Maverick hit above the oil level does little damage. Below the oil level, a 12-inch gusher spews out. If the stream torches off, the fire is easily extinguished.

There are two ways to kill a tanker with a Maverick. You can lock the missile onto a window on the ship's bridge into which the warhead will then penetrate trashing everything and everyone on the bridge. That will immobilize the tanker for quite some time. However, if you are concerned about killing non-combatant civilians who are just doing their jobs, and you should be, there is another, more humane tactic to employ. Oil tankers are single rudder, single screw ships. An attack from the stern usually disables the ship, rendering it un-steerable or dead in the water and leaving the crew alive but frustrated.

Years later, when I worked for Hughes Aircraft Company, the inventor/producer of the Maverick, I received a call from Egypt at home at our big Sunday brunch. Sunday is a work day in the middle east. The Egyptian Air Force was asking how to attack tankers with Mavericks. I gave the caller a 30-minute version of the paragraph just above. My then in-laws were visiting. My father-in-law, who was a really cool guy, remarked after I hung up, "Now there's a conversation you don't hear every day!"

No matter, it was good to hear from the intel folks that our training paid off.

Phil Comstock went on to command a flying squadron in the USAF, quite an achievement at the time for a navigator. Tom "Fireplug" Hood survived when the T-38 he was piloting came apart under high G loading. Tom parachuted into the Philippine Sea and was picked up. After leaving the Air Force, Mike VanWagenen was killed when the home-built aircraft he was testing broke up near Lake Tahoe. A year later, another ex-FWS IP and friend, Joe Henderson, lost his life also near Tahoe in a crash of the same under-development and under-designed homebuilt jet. The fatal-wreck aircraft was supposed to be the most advanced homebuilt ever, capable of over Mach one. It seems that a supersonic kit plane represents a bridge too far. General Kathami died in an ultra-light aircraft crash over north Teheran. He had refused to leave the country and desert his command when the fanatical mullahs took over. Sabotage was rumored. One of the Ayatollah Khomeini's alocyotes supposedly clipped some control cables, but nothing was ever proven as no formal accident investigation was ever allowed to proceed. That tells you something. Jalal Payami was killed when his F-5 flew into a flock of birds. The light weight fighter had a light weight windscreen unable to resist the impact of a large bird.

But what of the pretty Persian nurse? Nothing ever came of the sensuous invitation she extended. I never followed up despite her obvious attractiveness and availability. To have done so would have been so wrong on so many levels.

CHAPTER EIGHTEEN
US NAVY FIGHTER WEAPONS SCHOOL 1973

TOPGUN, an Outfit with No Guns

Slowly, light dawned over desks scattered in offices throughout the Pentagon and at the headquarters of the Tactical Air Command, TAC. Tactical thinkers of the USAF and of the USN began to realize learning air combat maneuvering by pitting F-4s against F-4s was no way to learn how to fight very dissimilar aircraft such as MiGs. Our kill ratio in the Vietnam War's later stages suffered for a lack of realistic training. Men were dying because they didn't know what they were doing. The brass was under pressure to do something about it.

The Navy got there first. They established a unit, the US Navy Fighter Weapons School (TOPGUN) at Miramar Naval Air Station just north of San Diego, CA. The mini-squadron was comprised of the best air-to-air jocks available. The headliners were, of course, Lt. Randy "Duke" Cunningham and his RIO, Lt. Willie "Irish" Driscoll. These two crewmates shot down five Mig-17s with Sidewinder heat-seeking missiles over North Vietnam, the first American jet aces since the Korean War.

Early in the year, I had just returned from a three-month staff college in Alabama, the Squadron Officers School, where I learned joined-up writing. The school was academic classroom training only, no flying. After two re-qual flights in the F-4, the USAF FWS sent me to the Navy counterpart. Great, I'd flown a grand total of two sorties in three months. Now I'm going up against an ace and guys who live and breathe air combat daily. Before leaving for Alabama, I transferred to the air-to-air flight at Nellis. I was supposed to bring back the inside scoop on what the Navy was doing right, if anything.

To simulate MiG-17s, the Navy took a few A-4 Skyhawk subsonic ground attack jets and stripped them of all items not needed for air combat. With no nose wheel steering, no radars, no guns, no drop tanks, no gunsights, and mounting the largest jet engine that would fit, the A-4 "Mongoose" aircraft were the hottest A-4s ever built. The leading-edge slats on the wings were bolted up and locked for easier handling at the cost of a higher landing speed. The jets were an airframe, engine, and radio, nothing else. I attended A-4 ground school for a week at El Toro Marine Corps Air Station, CA. Then I got a five-hop check out in the two-seat TA-4J at Miramar. The plan was for another Nellis jock, Major Ralph Schneider, and I to go through the USN FWS course as adversary pilots flying only the A-4.

For some reason, I hit it off with "Duke" Cunningham. He volunteered to check me out in air-to-air combat in the A-4, a plane originally designed for ground attack/close air support. The Mongoose was fun to fly, simple, honest, straightforward, and boasted of a superior thrust-to-weight ratio. It turned well and accelerated strongly until about .9 Mach when it ran into a wall of compressibility. Visibility from the cockpit was good, better than the F-4 once you actually got into the cockpit. It wasn't as tight as the F-104 but close. Cunningham's lessons consisted of a formation take-off and climb out to the practice area over the Pacific west of Miramar, which is near the beach. We'd turn 90 degrees away from each other then turn back in---fight's on.

This was the first time I flew a single-engine jet airplane, and over the ocean at that. It was a little unnerving, but I soon got used to it. At least I didn't have to try landing it on a boat. Duke and I enjoyed some epic air battles with very few "kill" calls, although I have to admit I did seek refuge in the sun a few times to negate a simulated heat-seeking sidewinder shot.

On my last checkout sortie, I was determined to do well, to shine my ass. I noticed USN formation takeoffs tended to be in the "same way, same day" category. I made up my mind to show all the jocks at Miramar, of which there were legion, how the USAF does formation flying. I tucked my jet in tight with Duke's A-4 not quite overlapping wing tips, keeping it there until we were airborne and clear of the field. When I had a spare second, I retracted the landing gear--handle up. On the climb out I couldn't keep up with Cunningham. I started to lag behind him. The A-4 has no afterburner, so that remedy was unavailable. I looked down to check the engine gages and saw one main landing gear still extended, the other main and the nose gear were up and locked. The maximum gear down speed in the A-4 is 175 knots, 200 mph. The airspeed indicator read 225 KIAS, 260 mph. In flying tight formation, I had neglected the gear, trying to retract the gear above the max speed, now one main was hung. I called Randy. He confirmed the sorry situation. He told me to slow down, put the gear handle down and see what happened. All three gear came down and locked, with three green lights burning bright. That was enough for me to call it a day after over-speeding the gear by 60 KIAS. However, my flight leader told me to suck up the gear and let's go fight. Despite my misgivings, that's just what I did.

When we almost reached minimum fuel to get home, I told Duke I'd really like to see if the landing gear was OK, so he reluctantly led us back to Miramar. I got three green lights in the traffic pattern and asked Duke to visually check out the gear. That was a mistake. The control tower heard that and asked it we had gear problems. I said, "I'm not sure." That was another mistake. The tower, it must have been a slow day up there, declared an emergency, rolled the fire trucks and an ambulance, telling me to hold off trying to land until they scrambled an LSO out to the end of the runway. BFD!

The LSO, Landing Signals Officer, is a guy who stands on a platform on the side of an aircraft carrier, even with the touchdown zone. He controls the final approach path and coaches the pilots trying to land. He can wave off an unsafe approach. He also grades every landing. During WWII, the LSO wielded brightly colored ping-pong paddles used to signal a pilot to bank left, bank right, go around, or press on, then cut the power to touch down. In that era, the LSO was very important, those piston-engined fighters had poor visibility over the nose during landing. The long nose stuck up in the air at slow airspeeds. Also, this was before the angled deck carrier. Then, once you were committed to touch down, you had to land, no touch and goes. If your tailhook missed grabbing a cable stretched across the deck, you ended up in a barrier which resembled the net on a tennis court, only higher, much stronger, and procured by the US Government. Nowadays with angled decks if you miss a cable, you just go around and try again. The angled deck also allows touch and go training as well. In the USN, being an LSO is a career path, pilots specialize in LSO-ing.

As an aside, the Royal Navy, RN, who at that time flew the same aircraft at the USN, F-4K Phantoms, dispensed with the LSO position years ago. The Brits fly a circular pattern instead of the USN's straight-in final approach. In a tight left turn, they can keep the touchdown zone in close sight, rolling wings level just in time to touch down. The USN thinks LSOs are essential for flying safety, the RN thinks they are a waste of time. The USAF, including yours truly, doesn't give a damn.

I saw no benefit of having an LSO watch me land. What could he, on the ground, see that my wingman couldn't? I told the tower I was low on fuel. I was going to attempt a death-defying landing even if the LSO hadn't yet made the scene at the end of the runway. I landed without incident and without an LSO.

Looking back, this episode together with another to follow, should have taught me something about Duke Cunningham. At the time, I didn't see it, but I do now. More on this later.

Randy gave me a copy of a book, *Jonathon Livingston Seagull*, by Richard S. Bach, an ex-USAF fighter pilot. The book was an ode to the joy of flight with a seagull as the protagonist. It was on the New York Times bestseller list but had nothing whatsoever to do with fighter aviation. My favorite Bach book was, and is, *Stranger to the Ground*, about flying the F-84 Thunderjet in Europe. I recommend it to anyone who wants to know what it is like to strap on a jet fighter. There is a lesson in the wildly divergent choices of aviation books between Cunningham and myself, but I'll be dammed if I know what it is.

Once I checked out as an adversary pilot, I flew against fleet guys in their F-4s. At the USAF FWS, we furnished F-4Es for our students' convivence. The Navy had the students fly their own aircraft in from their home unit along with the vital maintainers and crew chiefs. This built home-unit cohesion, if the student's jet broke, the student didn't fly. When the jet was ready, so was the student. Sometimes this approach backfired.

In a two-versus-four hassle, another TOPGUN guy and I were fighting four student F-4s. I achieved a guns-tracking solution on one student and was about to call a "kill." Before I could press the mike button, I saw large pieces separate from the F-4, shiny sheets of metal that that fluttered, tumbled, and headed down to the Pacific Ocean. My first thought was, "Yikes! That's realistic training." Then, "Did I do that?"

The Phantom's horizontal stabilators, one on each side of the tail, angled down. Each was each made up of two segments. The inboard panels were of aluminum, the outboard halves, closest to the hot jet engine exhaust, were of heat-resistant stainless steel. Where the two halves joined, steel was bolted directly to aluminum. When two dissimilar metals are joined, electrolysis corrosion can occur, particularly in a salty, humid environment as onboard an aircraft carrier. The F-4 pilot, call sign "Jungle Jim," for his ripped muscles, tried to spoil my tracking solution by yanking a ton of Gs. The corroded joints failed and both stab tips left the aircraft. It was my one and only simulated gun kill.

The Navy jock returned to Miramar, landing very hot. With half of his stabs gone, he couldn't control the aircraft at high AOAs and slow speeds, He touched down at 180 KIAS, 210 mph. His tailhook picked up the midfield cable yanking the aircraft to a complete stop. No sweat.

On one sortie, The Leader of TOPGUN, Lt/Commander, later Admiral, Ron "Mugs" Mckeown and I were scheduled for air combat training with a flight of two F-8 Crusaders of the USN Naval Reserve unit based at Miramar. The reserve pilots were everyday civilians, usually airline pilots, who reported for a few day's duty, with perhaps seven or ten sorties a month, to fly the F-8. The Crusader was being phased out of the active-duty navy. The USN had a unique way of paying its reserve pilots. It didn't. The F-8 jocks got fighter flying time and accrued days for a military retirement pension and benefits, but no salary. Eventually, they could "get on regular" and draw pay for their reserve stints, but that status wasn't assured. I always said I got paid for being in the US Air Force, for enduring the haircuts, the marching, the constant moves, the discipline. The flying I did for free. The USN Crusader guys proved me right.

When the practice fight began, those airline pilots turned Mugs and I every which way but loose. They were really, really good. The F-8 earned the title, "MiG Master" for having the best kill ratio of any aircraft in SEA and I saw why. The whole engagement took place beneath a 1800-foot overcast out over the Pacific. Trying to shake an opponent, I managed to enter the cloud deck inverted. The natural tendency was to pull the nose down and to try to fly out of the clouds, but that was a good way to make a big, one-time only splash. I rolled wings level on the gages and set up a gentle descent back to the visual world. When I emerged from the overcast, the F-8 was still right behind me, only closer. The crafty Crusader driver knew what I would do and waited for me to appear again in his 12 O'clock.

The Navy called the F-8 "The Last of the Gunfighters" as its primary weapon was four 20mm cannons. The Crusader also wielded Sidewinder missiles when out of gun range.

All Phantoms of that era wielded two air-to-air missiles; the short-range, heat-seeking AIM-9 Sidewinder for within visual range fights and the medium-range, radar-guided AIM-7 Sparrow. Both were developed by the US Navy.

The Sidewinder was cheap, reliable, and simple to employ. It had been in combat since the 1950s, notably with the Taiwan Chinese Air Force who notched up its first kill, a MiG-15 from the Peoples Liberation Army Air Force. Yes, that's what the Chicoms call it.

The Sparrow earned a rotten reputation among fighter jocks. It required the launch aircraft to illuminate the target with its fire control radar until the missile impacted the target. No fair launching and leaving. Total weapons system reliability comprised of; air crews, radars, and missiles, scored poorly. Half the missiles launched in early SEA combat were duds. The USAF had a saying, "What's the best way to employ the Sparrow? Jettison the lot, ridding the aircraft of 2000 pounds of dead weight." However, the Sparrow offered our only capability for beyond-visual-range, night, or bad weather combat.

For reasons best known to themselves, the Navy jocks focused on close-in combat with Sidewinders. Their F-4 aircraft never employed effective guns despite calling their FWS "TOPGUN." I suspect "TOP MISSILE" lacked panache. When the USN FWS began operations, attendance by fleet jocks was low. No one knew what the school was for. Its original name was a dull bureaucratic moniker and few volunteered to attend. The commander at the time changed the name to TOPGUN and guys lined up trying to get in. It's all about the branding, Baby! By the time I got there, the school was famous for expert Sidewinder employment tactics.

Randy Cunningham was an expert at this twisting, turning, climbing, diving, high-G environment. All his five MiG kills were with Sidewinders against MiG-17s. That's what the USN did and that's what they primarily taught at TOPGUN. Sparrow employment was an afterthought both in the classroom and in the air.

A well-worn cliché states short-range air-to-air combat is like a knife fight in a phone booth. Remember phone booths? In such a conflict, not having a gun on the aircraft is like conducting the imaginary phone booth fracas armed only with a broadsword.

The USAF took another path. We focused on making Sparrows work with increased training and better radar maintenance along with improved treatment of the missiles themselves. A training/test program was set up at Clark AFB, PI. Aircrews, their aircraft, and their missiles participated in Operation Combat Sage. Over time the AIM-7, the crews, and the F-4s improved. Shortly after Duke Cunningham returned to the States, USAF Captain Steve Ritchie and two GIBs, Lt. Jeffery Feinstein and Lt. Chuck Bellevue, became MiG aces. All Ritchie's five kills were with the Sparrow against the more advanced MiG-21. Go figure.

At Nellis and at Miramar, I flew with and against both Cunningham and Ritchie, probably the only fighter pilot to do so. At the time and even now, I considered Steve to be the superior aviator. He could do it all well, air-to-air, air-to-ground, short-range, long-range air combat. While Duke reigned as king in the Sidewinder arena, he was the first to tell you he knew zip about guns. Ritchie also served as a fast FAC in training FWS students. Cunningham considered bombing missions only as a way to get to the war to then look for MiGs. He told me once about a mission over North Vietnam where a flight of two USN F-4s loaded with dumb bombs got a call from the ship about MiGs in the general area. Duke marveled that the USN guys continued on their assigned mission. They didn't jettison the bombs and transition into the air-to-air mode. So much for military orders according to Duke.

At TOPGUN, I overheard Cunningham in conversation with another instructor. I think it was Winston Copeland. They had a contest going to see who could do a split S at the lowest altitude. In a split S, you fly straight and level, roll inverted, then pull down vertically through the second half of a loop. Duke said he did one starting at 2000 feet over the ocean. The next step was 1900 feet, then 1800. There were only two ways this contest would end; someone would scare themselves so badly by barely missing the wavetops, that he would withdraw. Or, someone would hit the water. I thought to myself this game is idiotic, risking it all for empty bragging rights in the crew room.

Looking back, I can see now that Randy Cunningham was addicted to adrenaline, hooked on risky behavior. He showed me he could disregard flying safety, my flying safety, telling me to suck up my landing gear which was of questionable integrity. The split S duel showed another red flag of his approach to life and flying which are sometimes the same thing.

At the Miramar O Club bar, Cunningham told me the Chief of Naval Operations, the CNO, promised him a choice of one of two follow-on assignments after TOPGUN; fly with the Blue Angles or serve in the USN's liaison office to Congress. I learned that later during the meeting, Duke had intended to tell the CNO he thought the Navy Cross medals he and Driscoll were awarded for becoming the first, and only, USN aces since Korea and for shooting down three MiGs on one sortie should be upgraded to the Congressional Medal of Honor, the CMH. The leader of TOPGUN at the time, Commander, later Admiral, Dave Frost told Cunningham if he lobbied for the CMH, that he, Dave Frost, would drum Cunningham out of the US Navy after personally strangling him.

We all know how this story played out. Cunningham went to Washington and began roaming the halls of Congress. He resigned from the Navy to run for Congress himself and got elected to the House of Representatives from the congressional district containing Miramar NAS. He later was convicted of taking bribes, spending four years in the federal pen. The decisive factor in his case was a list of rates, in dollars, of various types of illegal activities he would undertake for dirty money. This list lay in plain sight on his desk when the FBI came calling. No one not addicted to risk would have done such a thing. An alternative explanation is that he was sick of what and who he had become. Subconsciously he wanted to be caught.

The word is that after prison, he moved back to his home state of Missouri and cleaned up his act. He lobbies for prison reform, natch. He also does voluntary community service. I'm glad he straightened himself out. I enjoyed flying with Duke Cunningham. I learned a lot from him. He was also a great guy to be around. I can see where he would be a good retail politician. I wish him the best now.

Later the TOPGUN school acquired aircraft capable of simulating more advanced MiGs; the F-5 Freedom Fighter and the F-16 Viper. The USAF, not to be outdone, acquired through covert means, a squadron of real MiGs which our guys used to train USAF, USMC, and USN pilots. The history of this unit, located in restricted Area 51 desert north of Nellis AFB, is told in a book, *America's Secret MiG Squadron*, IBSN-13 #178-1899089760 by my good friend and mate in various squadrons, Colonel Gailard Peck Jr.

Having learned all I could stand from the US Navy, I returned to Nellis hell-bent on improving our own training, which needed it.

CHAPTER NINETEEN
WIN SOME, LOSE SOME

Some are Rained Out, the Rest are Fixed

When Steve Ritchie shot down his fifth MiG-21 over North Vietnam, he was ordered back to the States, to Washington DC, to meet and greet the great and the good in the Pentagon and the press. On his way to the world inside the Beltway, Steve stopped in at the FWS at Nellis AFB. His purpose: to find out what we needed, what should he tell the Chief of Staff of the USAF, the Commander of Tactical Air Command, TAC, and various other horse-holders, desk jockeys, and professional staff officers he would brief. He didn't plan on asking the Chief for the Congressional Medal of Honor.

Our message to the Air Force poohbahs, passed through Steve, was we needed an aggressor force, using dissimilar aircraft, like the USN operated at TOPGUN. Of course, having the Navy get there first helped grease the rival bureaucracy's skids. The first T-38 appeared on the Nellis ramp two weeks later, the start of an aggressor program. The USAF generals decided to TAKE the lead over the Navy. Who knew? Instead of a minimum schoolhouse operation, the USAF would commission a separate and dedicated full squadron with its own pilots, aircraft, shoulder patch, and all the accouterments of a USAF fighter squadron.

The aggressor squadron formed up and slowly the concept spread throughout the tactical air forces with other aggressors flying out of other bases. These squadrons eventually acquired aircraft more capable than the T-38. F-16s and F-15s were painted in MiG regalia and were flown by a succession of pilots chosen for their air-to-air expertise. Being an aggressor pilot became a minor career path. These guys, and gals, steeped themselves in Russian, Chinese, and Korean tactics and tried to fly and fight like the Bad Guys. They also learned to keep their egos in check, always difficult for fighter pilots. Instead of fighting to win, they learned to fly to teach, engaging to instruct. Now, most aggressor pilots are civilian contractors. They fly a wide variety of dissimilar aircraft; French Mirages and F1s, Swedish Drakens, what have you. The pilots are always retired or resigned jocks from the USN, USAF, and USMC. Not a bad retirement job, pretending to be a MiG pilot.

When I returned from TOPGUN, squadron mate Dave Smith and I revised the FWS air-to-air tactics manual. We tried to update the info therein with lessons learned at TTOGUN and in SEA combat. However, what we needed involved a complete re-think resulting in a complete re-write. At the time, we were still flying and teaching formations and tactics from the Korean War, 20 years in the past. Those ideas were themselves adopted from formations and tactics flown in WWII. In that long-ago conflict, Colonel "Hub" Zemke and the 59th Fighter Group, the original "Wolfpack," developed the Finger Four formation where the basic fighter unit, four aircraft, flew in an orientation identified by the positions of your fingertips. This worked well for the P-47 Thunderbolt propeller-driven fighters of the day.

In Korea, the F-86 Sabrejets modified the finger four into the Fluid Four. To simulate this alignment split your four fingers in a wide vee between your middle finger and ring finger. Also, the ring and little fingers could switch sides in flight with the first two. This is painful to do with real fingers and only slightly less hard to accomplish with real aircraft.

The F-86 was an aircraft with half the size, half the speed, and about half the turn radius of the F-4. It was armed with guns, not missiles. The F-4 we were flying was twice as big, over twice as fast, and with twice the turn radius. The Phantom initially wielded only missiles, no guns. It had made perfect sense to somebody in charge to use the same formations and tactics as the P-47 and F-86 while flying a wildly dissimilar aircraft.

It must be noted that late in the Vietnam War, the F-4E appeared with its internal and infernal 20 mm gatling gun, the same gun originally installed in the F-104. My good friend and squadron mate, Jim Beaty, stitched a MiG-21 from nose to tale with his F-4E's gun. Jim's throttles were in full afterburner, the aircraft flying well over Mach one at the time, moving with the speed of heat. It was probably the world's first and only supersonic gun kill. The MiG blew up like expensive fireworks. Jim pulled 9 Gs avoiding the resulting fireball when the aircraft came back subsonic, blacking him and his GIB out cold. They thought they were dead but instead came back heroes.

Slightly later, Major, later Colonel, Gail Peck, another FWS squadron mate, did indeed re-write the air-to-air tactics manual starting from a clean sheet of paper. He incorporated his experiences as the squadron commander of the USAF's covert collection of MiG-17s and MiG-21s. Gail interviewed as many fighter aces from the past as he could find hoping to uncover some universal and unchanging truths about air combat. He even found a (very) old fighter pilot from WWI living in Las Vegas and picked his brain as well. The old guy's advice, "Watch out for the Hun in the Sun" didn't make it into the finished book. After my partial re-write, it wasn't all work for me at the Fighter Weapons School.

To my very great surprise, I got invited to try out for the United States Air Force Aerial Demonstration Team, the Thunderbirds. That represented a pie-in-the-sky lifetime goal of mine. I was stoked to get the opportunity and determined to make the best impression I could. I went on a short trip with the team to airshows somewhere in Indiana; Kokomo I think, then Saint Louis, Missouri: and the USAF Academy in Colorado Springs, CO. This tag-along was easy to do as the Thunderbirds were flying the F-4 with room for two. I flew with Major Joe Howard, the Right Wing in the formation. Joe was a nice guy but didn't have much to say in the cockpit.

The formation flying the team exhibited was very tight, with wingtips overlapping at times and #4, the Slot Man, Tom Gibbs, tucked in so tight in the diamond formation's slot the tail of his jet was colored black by soot from the Leader's exhaust. Their Phantoms were modified for airshows, painted red, white, and blue with the outline of a "Thunderbird" on the bellies. I never found out where the mythical bird's outline came from. The radars had been removed and in the nose's cavity was mounted a baggage compartment for carry-on luggage.

Smoke, which made for spectacular airshows, was generated by used engine oil carried in a converted tank # seven in the tail and sprayed into the hot jet exhaust to produce a fluffy trail. Lighting the afterburner erased the smoke trail so its use during close formation by an individual pilot was discouraged as that left a gap in the four continuous white streaks. Any bobble or momentary dip, called a "yug," also put a wave in the smoke trail. The offending pilot would be chastised during the post-show debrief after watching a video recording made of the performance.

Flying formation aerobatics of the sort displayed by the Thunderbirds and their counterparts of the USN, the Blue Angels, requires a pilot to re-orient himself in the world. Solo acrobatics are flown with the earth below as a reference. To perform a loop, for example, you start with the aircraft's nose on, and its wings level with, the horizon. Then you trace a vertical circle perpendicular to the earth ending up with the nose and wings in their original position relative to the horizon. In a formation, your reference changes to the leader's aircraft. You maintain that relationship no matter where the horizon or the earth happens to be during the maneuver.

One aspect of the Thunderbirds approach to show biz and formation flying puzzled me then and still does today. When the T-Birds flew the F-100 Super Sabre, the "Hun" evidently had a lot of slop in the flight control system. To eliminate control stick's dead zone, those pilots rolled in nose-down trim to take up the slack. Every jet of that era mounted a trim button, a "coolie hat" on top of the stick. This allowed pilots to balance out the feedback forces fed into the control system by wildly varying airspeeds, 130 KIAS to well over Mach Two. Over time, the team, probably under the influence of machismo competition, used full nose-down trim. This gave the feeling of holding the aircraft up in the air with your right arm. This nonsensical tradition carried over into the F-4. I found it hard to believe Thunderbird airplanes with their superb maintenance had any slop in the stick.

At Georgia Tech, I attended a briefing put on by the T- Bird pilots, then in the F-100. They boasted of using full nose down trim, saying it made their formation flying smoother. It also drew comments from Flight Surgeons during annual flight physical exams about having their right arms more muscular than their lefts. Welcome to the one-armed gun show.

Kinematically, this made no sense. It is difficult to make the small, precise movements with your hands and arms required by close formation flying while simultaneously straining with your biceps. It would be like trying to sign your name with a pen taped to a 10-pound bar bell. But Thunderbird tradition demanded full nose-down trim, at least publicly. I had my doubts whether they actually used it. When I tried it, my formation flying didn't get smoother. It went to Hell. Now in the F-16 aircraft, the Thunderbird tradition of full nose-down trim is NOT APPLICABLE. The Viper's control stick doesn't move, it is a force transducer instructing the computers actually flying the aircraft. No trim button, no ripped right arms.

One aspect of the Thunderbird's operation I hadn't anticipated was the relentless social life. Everywhere we stopped we were presented with a series of receptions, press briefings, meet-and-greets, and the occasional party. I expected the flying to predominate but at least half the team's mission involved public relations, recruiting, and community outreach. The operative instruction was, "Pace yourself, it's only Wednesday." When I returned home to Nellis, I was exhausted.

Also on the trip was painter Keith Ferris. He traveled with the ground crew in the C-130 "Hercules" transport which always accompanies the team. Keith, a really nice guy, is famous for painting aerial scenes which are true to life and are fantastically accurate in every detail; the lighting, the aircraft, the markings, the weather. He was disparaged by the art community as nothing more than an illustrator, a talented illustrator, but not a real, sensitive artist. However, no one wants an Impressionist's treatment of air combat with fuzzy, smeared images. Ferris later painted two whole walls of the Smithsonian Air & Space Museum on the Mall in Washington. One scene is a tableau of a B-17 high over Germany, among icy contrails. It gives you chills to see it. I later bought a print of Keith's painting of Colonel Robin Olds shooting down a MiG-21 over North Vietnam. It's on my "I love me" wall of military awards and plaques in our home basement "entertainment complex."

The last event on the try-out agenda was a stress interview by all seven flying team members. There were three of us rookies trying for one slot. The interview's purpose was to determine how you handled yourself under verbal pressure, as in a hostile press interview, as well as to see if your attitude fit in with Thunderbird culture. The leader, Lt/Col, later Lt/General Tom Swalm led the proceedings flanked by his team members. The interviewee, that would be me, was seated in a lone chair, very alone, in front of the interview board. I was the first candidate to be inquisitioned.

I thought I acquitted myself fairly well during the trip. I refrained from ordering Beaujolais red wine to drink with my sole meuniere fish course. I didn't make a pass at any unattached, attractive women. I hadn't waved my hands, over-G-ing my wrist watch, while explaining flying maneuvers.

The interview wasn't too stressful. I've never had any trouble with public speaking. The final, and most important question, came from the Leader/Commander himself:

"Ed, you've flown with the team this week and you've seen what we do in the air. Do you think you can hack the flying aspects of being a Thunderbird?"

There were three possible replies to this question:

The "A" answer would have been, "I don't see how I could ever achieve the degree of proficiency displayed by you master aviators."

The "B" reply would have been, "If I bust my tail, work hard, concentrate on my formation flying, I just might hack the program."

I chose the "D-minus" answer, "The flying didn't look all that hard to me," or words to that effect. I didn't mention full nose-down trim.

Tom Swalm looked up at the door to the interview room as if to say, "Next."

I didn't make the team. But just being considered scored a career highlight. As it turned out, I did participate in a program which ultimately proved to be much more important to the USAF than spraying white smoke over adoring crowds at air shows.

As the Vietnam War wound down, the debriefing, analysis, and finger-pointing began. The "Who's to blame?" process wasn't pretty. Leaving aside the failures on the ground in South Vietnam and the counter-productive air campaigns in the out-country war, the judgement on our training was brutal. We didn't send guys to the war trained for the challenges they would find there. Early in the conflict fighter squadrons were composed of old heads, guys who had seen the bright lights and had heard the loud noises in Korea. Some even flew and fought in WWII. These jocks, if they hadn't fought in a real war, were trained by those who had. Their performance was as good as could be expected under the idiotic Rules of Engagement the LBJ White House imposed and the chain of command passively handed down to the poor sods who had to follow them. Some of these old pros, like Major Robbie Risner, a F-105 pilot, got their mugs on the cover of Time magazine.

As the war ground on, the average fighter pilot's experience level went down while the experience level of the defenders in North Vietnam and Laos went up. Losses mounted. MiGs were shooting down our guys and Surface to Air Missiles, SAMs, were introduced, taking their toll of our pilots and aircrews. Bombing pauses over North Vietnam provided breaks in the carnage, but the threat remained active.

The data was clear, pilot losses tended very strongly to occur during a fighter pilot's first ten missions. After an initial trial-by-fire, a new guy had a much better chance of surviving a full year's tour, or 100 missions, whichever came first. As a personal reminder to me, my wife's first husband and my daughter's birth father, Lt. Bob Scott, was lost on his third combat sortie. In effect, we were letting the enemy do our instruction for us. Air combat shouldn't require total on-the-job training. We needed to do better.

One night in Las Vegas, the FWS air-to-air flight threw a party at the bachelor pad occupied by Gail Peck, later a full Colonel, and Joe Hurd, later a Lt. General. Major Moody Suter, later another Colonel, and me, later a civilian. We all attended along with several wives. Suter reigned as our fearless leader. He had a hidden agenda for the gathering. After a few, OK more than a few, adult beverages, we were discussing the sad training situation outlined above. Moody postulated a requirement; how to get a fighter pilot those vital first ten stressful sorties without relying on the Bad Guys to provide the education.

We kicked the idea around among us four. Moody had a knack for throwing out a concept and then leading a discussion at the end of which all the participants would believe they had thought of the concept on their own. This was a skilled way to get buy-in. Listening to Moody Suter's ideas was like breeding horses, only without anyone getting screwed. Say you breed ten foals, raise, and train them. You lose money on eight. The ninth colt breaks even financially. The tenth has great potential and pays the bills for the others. If Moody had ten ideas, eight would be unworkable, bordering on wacky. The ninth might have potential. The tenth would be a world-changer. He was a legendary thinker about tactical aviation. His professional life was the subject of magazine articles. That night in Vegas, he won the National Championship Horse Show.

We conceived replicating a high-threat environment on the extensive Nellis AFB gunnery ranges. The aggressor squadron could provide Red Air opposition. We'd get fake radar emitters to light up cockpit radar warning receivers. The war game would be large-scale with many aircraft, maybe even with aerial refueling. Guys would fly a part of a strike package, with 12-16 aircraft. The targets would be realistic as well, all tactical complexes, not bulldozed circles in the desert.

After much conversation and even more waving of hands, we wrote the idea down on, what else, a cocktail napkin, actually several napkins. Moody Suter soon was reassigned to the Pentagon where he preached the gospel of what we had wrought that night. The result was Red Flag, still in robust operation today. It is the largest, most realistic air combat war game/training exercise in the world. Numerous allied air forces participate as do bombers, tankers, electronic countermeasures aircraft and search-and-rescue forces. A French Mirage might engage an aggressor F-16 to protect a USAF B-1B Lancer bomber supported by USN jamming aircraft. The whole scene is monitored and recorded for debriefing back at Red Flag HQ. Mission debriefs have run into the late-night hours.

As I look back on my USAF flying career, I take pride in two accomplishments: the introduction of Precision-Guided Munitions, PGMs, and the genesis of Red Flag. I played a very minor role in each of these developments but that doesn't prevent me from bragging about them.

PGM's allow pinpoint attacks, limiting collateral damage. Red Flag helps aviators like Bob Scott a better chance of living to see their daughters grow up.

The year after I tried out for the Thunderbirds, Major Joe Howard was killed during an airshow at Dulles Airport outside of Washington, DC. His F-4 lost all hydraulic power to the flight controls and entered a flat spin. Joe ejected at low altitude, the aircraft impacting beneath him, The resulting fireball and mushroom cloud consumed his parachute, dropping him into the flames.

Before my tour at Nellis AFBV and the USAF Fighter Weapons School ended, I had the opportunity to improve my bad weather flying skills, which since leaving Thailand, had atrophied to virtually non-existent in the always-clear desert climate of Las Vegas.

CHAPTER TWENTY
ADVENTURES IN THE
LAND OF ZION

Dashing Through the Snow

I was scheduled to ferry an aircraft from Nellis to the repair depot at Hill AFB, Ogden, Utah. The tired jet was due for Inspection and Repair As Necessary, IRAN. It would be disassembled, inspected, repaired as necessary, then repainted and returned to active duty. IRAN in Utah had nothing to do with the country of Iran where the jets were brand new and didn't need extensive maintenance.

The weather forecast for Hill AFB wasn't sparkling. A major winter snow storm was bearing down on the base but it wasn't likely to hit for another hour-and-a-half or two hours. Or so the pretty weather lady, a Lt., said when the GIB and I filed the flight plan at Base Operations. We hustled to get airborne and lit out for Utah, the Land of Zion, as the locals called it.

A clean F-4, no drop tanks or ordnance, cruises most efficiently at altitude at .92 Mach, over nine-tenths the speed of sound. This is the same speed an older Boeing 747 Jumbo Jet cruises at. Why is beyond me. Evidently, the idea is to get where you are going quickly before you can run out of gas. We attempted to do just that. The GIB calculated our enroute go-no-go point. That is the time in the flight where we would not have enough fuel to return to Nellis and would be committed to land at Hill. At this decision point, I called on the radio for a weather update. The Air Traffic Control, ATC, controller told us the weather in the Ogden area remained workable but the storm was nearing. Ten minutes later, the storm hit the base. The FAA guy had probably been reading an hour-old report. To make things worse, ATC told us Hill AFB would be closing to all traffic shortly. I replied they could close the base if they wanted to, but we were committed to land there, no matter what.

Base weather reported a 500-foot ceiling with one-to-two miles visibility in blowing snow when we began our let-down. I re-acquainted myself with the cockpit blind-flying instrument displays while transiting through bumpy clouds. Approach Control gave us excellent vectors to the runway rolling us out on the final approach heading. The GIB picked up the runway's radar reflectors, two on each side of the touchdown zone, on the aircraft's air intercept radar. He refined our heading and suggested what altitude would be appropriate and reminded me to extend the landing gear and flaps. No fancy automated instrument landing aides in the ol' F-4. When we emerged from the overcast, the we were on the correct heading and the runway lay directly ahead. At least I assumed the white nothingness on the ground visible out the windscreen was the runway. The strip was totally covered with inches of fresh snow. I picked the area which looked to be the flattest to land on.

I told myself this would be like landing during a torrential monsoon rain storm on a narrow runway in Thailand. I should use the same techniques. I put out the drag chute while still in the air over the overrun. Then I plunked the aircraft solidly down on what I assumed to be the "piano keys," the black and white rectangles painted on the threshold but hidden by a blanket of the white stuff. Steering the aircraft down the centerline with the ailerons and ignoring the nosewheel steering, I let the anti-skid system work the wheel brakes.

Hill AFB has a 10,000-foot runway and we used 9,950 feet of it stopping the jet in the slippery ice and snow. I could have dropped the tail hook and picked up the mid-field barrier, an arresting cable stretched across the concrete halfway down the runway. That would have stopped us like Lt. Randy Cunningham picking up the #3 wire while landing back aboard the USS Constellation. However, that plan would have entailed the ground crew having to reset the barrier in the blizzard, not a fun job for them. Also, I felt confident, perhaps overly-so, in my ability to get us stopped in time.

After dropping the big yellow drag chute in the de-arm area, we tailed the blue "Follow Me" truck to the parking ramp. The tarmac looked more like the Montreal Canadiens' hockey rink, only without the icing lines and without goal nets. The truck stopped and an airman jumped out to marshal us into our parking slot. How he could tell where it lay under the snow wasn't apparent. I pointed the aircraft at the young guy who held up the international hand sign for "stop" by crossing his forearms in an X in front of his face.

I applied the wheel brakes, to little effect. The Phantom continued ahead at a walking pace. A jet engine generates significant thrust even when at idle. The two idling J-79s were propelling the jet forward. I should have shut down one engine while taxing in to reduce our ground speed but the thought never crossed my mind. The wheels were locked, the anti-skid doesn't work at very low speeds, and the nose wheel steering was ineffective. In desperation, I slammed both throttles rearward into the "off" position.

The ground crew member saw the aircraft continuing toward him relentlessly. The nose pointed at his chest, with no sign of halting its forward progress. From the cockpit, I could see his eyes widen and his jaw drop. Hearing me shut down the engines alerted him to the possibility I was no longer in complete command of my aircraft. I was only along for the ride on the world's largest camouflaged toboggan. He turned to run to one side but instead slipped and fell, disappearing under the approaching black nose cone. Yikes! I was about to become the first pilot to run down a pedestrian with a supersonic jet. A second or two later, I saw him rolling in the snow out from under the radome, evading the dual nose wheels. At this point, I had played all my cards, badly. The GIB and I were helpless spectators.

Next up on the icy obstacle course loomed the parked truck. The pitot tube on the tip of the nose was about to spear the truck like a chicken in a fryer. Slowly, the runaway Phantom, its engines wound down now to silence, slid to a stop with the pitot tube less than three feet from the vehicle. We opened the canopies, climbing down as the airman dusted the snow off his winter parka. All three of us acted as if nothing unusual had happened and no catastrophe had almost occurred.

MEMO TO SELF: DO NOT VOLUNTEER FOR DUTY IN THE ALASKAN AIR COMMAND!

A few weeks later, my weather-related adventures continued. All pilots in the FWS were required to practice aerial refueling, once in the daytime, once at night, every six months. For those of us who had recently served in SEA, this task was a piece of cake. During our combat tours we had refueled from a tanker dozens, maybe hundreds, of times. It is a skill which does not erode with time. However, learning to aerial refuel was the hardest skill I ever learned. I only succeeded by telling myself I would get the hang of it or die trying, literally. Learning from the F-4's back seat didn't help matters, but eventually, I got very good at it from either cockpit.

These aerial refueling missions were not part of the FWS curriculum, so we would launch a four-ship formation with only FWS IPs on board. It has been rumored, but not confirmed, that the day/night requirement was sometimes filled by a late afternoon flight. It could have been possible to conduct one set of four refuelings in the daytime, then hang about for a half-hour or so with the tanker until official sunset and then get four "night" plug-ins in the twilight. Maybe it happened that way, maybe not. In any case, these training missions somehow always seemed to be scheduled for late on a Friday, when we would have much rather been at the O Club stag bar instead on practicing what we already knew how to do.

The weather that afternoon appeared stinko with mid-winter snow storms in the refueling track over Utah with more hovering north of Nellis. We would have to refuel between layers of clouds. Refueling in a thunderstorm was STRICKLY PROHIBITED. But in SEA, I had refueled in a tropical monsoon because running out of gas was also frowned upon by the higher-ups. That time, the tanker crew let me hook up despite the regulations. Those guys were dedicated and they did what they had to do. It wasn't uncommon for a fighter wing to recommend a tanker crew for a heroism medal while the Strategic Air Command, SAC, processed disciplinary measures for the same crew for the same action. During the stormy refueling, Saint Elmo's Fire flowed over the F-4. Rivulets of bright green flames played along the canopy over my head like the fingers of a chartreuse hell. We were transferring thousands of gallons of jet fuel between aircraft while static electricity sparked over us. What could have possibly gone wrong? However, the FWS mission was over the Land of Zion, not the kingdom of Laos. Lightning wasn't an issue.

What was an issue was my GIB, or lack my thereof. An Air Force Academy cadet, a Zoomie. was strapped into the rear cockpit. During the summer between their junior and senior years, Cadets were sent out to the "Real Air Force" for a month to learn how it would be should they graduate. The mini-tours also served as a motivational experience. In the 414th, the cadets posted the flying schedule, answered the phone, filed paperwork, ran errands, and acquainted themselves with everyday life in a fighter squadron. As a reward, each got a ride in the back seat on a non-FWS sortie. My back-seater was an impressive young man, eager to learn. I gave him a detailed cockpit orientation, instructing him on how to align the inertial platform, work the radar, and change radio channels. He adsorbed the drink from a fire hose like a sponge. We launched as # Four in the flight led by ol' buddy Gail "Evil" Peck.

We would have to refuel over Utah between cloud layers, but first we had to find the tanker, which orbited in a race-track pattern impatiently awaiting our arrival. The KC-135 crew was probably as happy to be flying on late Friday afternoon as we were. I talked to the cadet, coaching him on operation of the air-to-air radar. He quickly illuminated and then obtained a lock-on to the tanker.

Instantly, I pressed the mike button and transmitted, "Four's tied," indicating we had found the tanker first, before any of the other three rated aviators in the other rear cockpits. I could hear the smiles from behind me through the intercom.

The refueling was routine as the weather worsened. When we started back to Nellis, the winter storm had descended on the Las Vegas valley. Night had fallen with a dark thud. As soon as Peck turned the formation back toward home base, we were in the clouds.

Flying close formation at night in the weather is tough. My sole reference was my immediate leader, # Three. His aircraft was my only visual link to the world around and below us. The throttles and controls stick moved almost imperceptibly in my Nomex-gloved hands in response to slight changes in our relative position vis-à-vis # Three. Three feet forward, four feet up, two feet out, then back in place. Impossible to take my eyes off his aircraft, no matter what the formation did.

The situation was ripe for a case of Spatial Disorientation, what the flight surgeons referred to as "spatial D." This is when your inner ears, which provide your sense of balance, are deceived by the motion and G-loading of the aircraft. Your body is telling you the world is in one orientation and your cockpit gauges tell you it's not; it's in another place. It is imperative to believe your gauges and not your ears. There have been several well-publicized cases of spatial D resulting in the deaths of celebrities: Kobe Bryant, the star basketball player, and the President's son, John F. Kennedy Jr., both met their maker due to cases of spatial D. Bryant's helicopter pilot became disoriented in the weather over Southern California. John-John augered in the twin-engined light plane he was piloting over the ocean off Massachusetts at night.

During the aforementioned episode of refueling in a thunderstorm over Laos, I was bouncing all over the place while taking on fuel. I was usually rock-solid on the boom but not on that night.

The GIB came up on the intercom, "Will you please settle down?"

I replied, "I think I'm doing pretty good for being in a ninety-degree bank." Spatial D had me but good.

Back over Nevada, with all my focus on maintaining my formation position, I was working my ass off. Peck was a smooth stick but the night clouds were bumpy with turbulence. As # Four, I was on the end of a crack-the-whip ride. Lead would bounce three feet, # Three would react, bouncing six feet. I would have to dampen out the excursions. This was definitely harder than flying with the Thunderbirds. That's because the ace aerial demo team almost never performs at night and in the weather.

We made it back to near Nellis without losing anyone out of the formation and Peck checked in with Vegas Approach Control requesting individual instrument let-downs. We would use the TACAN, TACtical Aid to Navigation, to shoot non-precision approaches. These maneuvers were called "non-precision" for good reasons. The TACAN provided range and bearing to a beacon on the airfield but no other information. Peck then put the formation, which had been in a finger-four orientation, into an echelon right. This prevented opening up a gap in the formation when he departed but gave me even more trouble as the crack-the-whiplash was now three aircraft long.

The protocols for individual approaches in the weather had been developed when most fighters were single-seat aircraft. The proscribed order was; Lead, #Two, #Three, and then #Four. That's because only the flight leader knew were the formation was. Everyone else was too busy flying formation to navigate. I expected Peck to adhere to the classic procedure. Of course, in the F-4, the GIB in each jet was supposed to maintain situational awareness and navigate. In our case, the right descent order should have been inverted, with # Four, that would be me, breaking off first as # Four usually had the least amount of fuel left after jockeying the throttles for half an hour. However, instead of a rated aviator in my rear cockpit, I had a Zoomie. I didn't even know where the ground was, much less the airfield. Peck told approach control # Four would shoot an approach first. Yikes!

At that time, instrument approaches were listed in four 5X9-inch paperback books, one for each quadrant of the USA. Each airfield with a published approach was represent on a single page. This page listed everything you needed to know about any sort of "blind-flying" let down including a graphic representation of the required flight path. In normal times, the GIB would read out the approach plate. I would attempt to follow his directions. I had a copy of the SW book, but it was buried deep in the map case next to the ejection seat. Another copy rested untouched in the rear cockpit.

I asked the AFA Cadet, "Do you know how to read a let-down book?" In the odd chance he had picked up some flight experience at the academy.

The reply came back, "Sir, we need a book to let down?" It would have been hilarious if I wasn't so twitched.

I should have taken out the approach plate before take-off and clipped it to my knee board, but I didn't. Hubris strikes again.

Three remedies to the problem were apparent: 1) I could have asked Peck, the flight leader, to penetrate first, in the classic order, which would have given me time when alone after the others had left to study up on the process. 2) I could have asked Vegas Approach Control for a radar vector to the airfield. Or, 3) I could try to hack the mission by myself. The first two courses of action would have entailed admitting on the radio I was inept and I needed outside help. No points for guessing which plan I embraced. If there ever was a situation which illustrated the driving imperatives of fighter pilots, that was it. Risk your life rather than admit failure or even worse, look foolish.

Peck had been a T-38 IP in the Air Training Command. He knew this instrument business like the back of his hand. I promptly forgotten most of it soon after getting my wings. He called Approach Control advising that # Four was ready to begin a descent and cleared me to depart the formation, all alone.

I remembered the race-track holding pattern for approaches to Nellis was located north of the Vegas Valley, over the mountains. The operative word being "mountains," mountains high enough to have s ski area at the top of one, Mount Charleston. Not the sort of terrain to get lost in while descending in the clouds. You could encounter a formation of cumulous ruckus.

I turned the jet ten degrees away from the formation which was instantly lost to sight in the dark and mist. Sweating bullets, I checked our altitude, airspeed, made sure we were wings level by the attitude indicator not by my lying senses, and that we were in level flight, not descending. I engaged the autopilot. "George" could fly the Phantom while I figured things out. I made sure the TACAN was locked on, turned up the cockpit lights, no need to preserve my night vision anymore, and frantically dug around in the map case for the let-down book. I finally found the right book and the correct page. Good ol' Gail had turned me loose right on track, all I had to do was to follow the graphic and written directions.

Finding Las Vegas at night was usually super easy. The Vegas valley was, and still is, a cauldron of neon glow, of search lights, of street lights, and of hotel/casinos illuminated by giant spot lights. The multi-colored aura was surrounded by a hundred miles of open, black desert in all directions. Even flying over the desert far from Sin City, you could follow the spider web of car headlights tracing out the few highways into town. Once over the valley, the Las Vegas Strip stood out like a blazing streak of neon, the great non-white way. But you had to be careful, remembering Nellis AFB was 10 miles to the northeast of the Strip or else you might try to land at Caesar's Palace like Evil Knievel.

This night, following the cockpit indications, we descended into the valley. The lights of Vegas lit up the clouds enveloping the Phantom. It was like flying in a bottle of milk. At about 1000 feet above the ground, we broached the bottom of the overcast to find the Nellis runway dead ahead. After landing, I quickly debriefed the Zoomie and split for the bar. I didn't trust myself to speak to Peck about his choice of descent order.

I often wondered what the AFA young man told his classmates about his ride in the back seat of an F-4 at night. Did he mention the need, not for speed, but for a book to be able to let down..

Little did I know at the time my new-found cold weather skill set would soon come in handy in the royal service of Her Royal Majesty, Elisabeth II, Queen of England.

CHAPTER TWENTY-ONE
A YANK IN THE ROYAL AIR FORCE

In Service for the Queen and Her Country

As my three-plus years as an instructor at the Fighter Weapons School drew to a close, I confronted a quandary; what next assignment to strive for. I served and flew near the top of what author Tom Wolfe called the pilot's "ziggurat" (look it up) of aviation in his book, *The Right Stuff*. I viewed a posting to a line fighter squadron as a step or two down. I was a senior captain, that lowly rank would not have offered me any chance to command a flight. I enjoyed instructing, but I viewed an assignment to the Air Training Command as more than two steps down accompanied by possible exile back to Texas.

I had always been intrigued by the idea of an exchange tour with an allied air force. Ever since the days of yore when American pilots flew in the Lafayette Escadrille with the French in WWI and the Eagle Squadron of the Royal Air Force in WWII, we have had flying slots in various other air forces. This grew into a formal exchange program in the 1950s. Guys from Canada, or Australia, or New Zealand or many other air arms, would fly and train with our squadrons and an equal number of our guys would go the opposite way to serve with the allies. As a qualified fighter weapons instructor, three possible assignments were offered to me by the rated assignment folks at the USAF personnel HQ. I could use my familiarity with the A-4 Skyhawk in the Royal New Zealand Air Force which flew the latest model "Scooter." The idea of living in New Zealand was interesting. But one look at a globe showed how my family and I would probably not see any of our relatives for the entire two-year tour. Kiwi land was ruled out.

Another opening appeared with the Royal Canadian Air Force flying the F-104. It would have been neat to fly the "Zipper" once again, but that stiletto of an aircraft was getting long in the tooth, soon to be obsolete. The RCAF used the Starfighter in a low-level ground attack role, not as the air defense fighter the jet was designed to be. Anyway, there was no way we wanted to live in a place called "Cold Lake, Alberta, Canada." The base was closer to the Artic Circle than to the US border. Despite the obvious appeal of living in France, my rudimentary command of the French language proved insufficiently fluent. That left the Royal Air Force, RAF, and their new Jaguar aircraft. That would have probably been my first choice anyway.

As an aside, the proper nomenclature for the RAF is the "Royal Air Force" not the "British Royal Air Force" or the "English Royal Air Force," or with any other modifier before th word "Royal." There are several other "Royal Air Forces" such as the aforementioned air arms in Canada and New Zealand or the Royal Australian Air Force, or the Royal Norwegian Air Force, but only one "Royal Air Force," full stop.

My wife, Pat, expressed serious reservations about the location of the proposed posting, on the north coast of Scotland, where the only things between us and the North Pole would be some oil rigs. At the time, the oil boom was just beginning in the North Sea and the financial benefits had yet to trickle down to Scotland. It owned the reputation of being remote and primitive. I prevailed but her premonition proved to be sadly accurate. The living in northern Scotland was austere and miserable, particularly compared to where we moved from, Las Vegas, NV.

I had always been intrigued by the RAF. As a kid and a young man, I read everything I could get my hands on about the Battle of Britain, fought in the summer and autumn skies of 1940. I knew the names of famous RAF legends and fighter pilots; Sir Douglas Bader, Pierre Klosterman, "Sailor" Moran, Geoffrey Quill, Trafford Leigh-Mallory (boo!), Johnnie Johnson, Sir Keith Parks (yea!), Robert Sanford-Tuck, and others. The opportunity to fly in the RAF like my heroes over-ruled my misgivings about living in the wilds of Scotland. I filled out the volunteer forms and received orders to report to the USAF/RAF Exchange Program at the US Embassy in London, England. There I in-briefed with the Colonel who ran the program from the Embassy.

Before I could report to my Jaguar unit, I needed to learn to speak proper English and grasp the subtilities of RAF procedures both in the air and on the ground. First up was a week at RAF Boscombe Down outside London. This is the Edwards AFB of the RAF, where they test experimental/developmental aircraft. My job wasn't to wring the rivets out of an X-plane but rather to get a handle on British flight terminology.

The instructional pace was relaxed. My classmates were all RAF officers returning from staff tours, working their way back into the cockpit.

Our residence was the Officers Mess. One thing I learned at Boscombe Down was most of the Officers Mess buildings in the RAF were built in the 1930s, all to the same plan. If you knew where the latrine, or more importantly the bar, was located in one, you knew them all. The vibe was of a genteel men's club with a formal dining room, smoking rooms, a wood-paneled bar, and an aura of faded glory. My first notion the RAF had fallen on hard times concerned transport from the Mess to our classroom. It was a 200–300-yard walk and most of us enjoyed the stroll over and back. However, one of our classmates was an Air Commodore, equivalent to a Brigadier General, a one-star in the USAF. Instead of the expected official staff car and maybe a driver, the AC was issued a bicycle which he dutifully pedaled back and forth.

I did learn the landing gear was the undercarriage, a touch-and-go was a roller, and afterburners were reheats. I also learned how to conduct myself as a gentleman in a RAF Officers Mess. That took some doing. We didn't play liar's dice at the bar. We played croquet on the lawn. The pool table didn't have pockets. It was for a game called "snooker." I don't think Paul Newman as Fast Eddie Felton ever played snooker.

After acclimatization at Boscombe Down, it was off for two weeks at RAF Leeming at North Allerton in Yorkshire for 10 flights in the Jet Provost. The Provost was the spitting image of a 1.25 scale T-37 Tweety Bird only with a single engine. Unlike the Tweet, the Jet Provost was fun to fly despite the side-by-side seating. My RAF IP was a good guy and let me do pretty much what I wanted. You could spin the Provost which was a lot of laughs unless the spin was inverted. That was disorientating but provided good training. I learned to talk to the RAF air traffic people and control tower chaps in terminology they could understand. You could even go cross-country in the Provost although it didn't take long to cross the country. The aircraft had a fitted set of leather luggage, called "paniers," for your clothes. Real class.

One night a group us from the Mess went into North Allerton to a classic British Pub, probably called "The Rose and Crown." The drinking laws were strict then as to the hours a pub could serve alcohol and stay open. At the proscribed hour, I think it was 2230, ten-thirty, the local Police Constable, PC, marched in respondent in full blue uniform. Evidently, he knew the publican as their exchange went something like this;

"Time, Jackie," said the PC.

"Right-O, Fred," came the reply from behind the bar as the lights went dim in the joint and the police officer spun on his polished heels and departed.

I stood up to leave, but my mates motioned me to sit back down and be quiet. We sat in the semi-darkness for about 10-15 minutes sipping on the last of our drinks. Then the door opened and the PC re-entered, only in civilian clothes this time. The lights came back on and we continued drinking with the PC, who having done his job, was now off-duty.

After another short stay, too short, in London, I caught a train to Elgin, Scotland. The journey took all day, changing in Inverness, Scotland. My first clue that "Toto, I don't think we're in Kansas anymore," was on the train. We crossed Hadrian's Wall, the traditional border between civilized England and wild Caledonia, or Scotland. The stone fence was not visible from the train. Two older Scots gentlemen boarded and sat across from me. They struck up an aminated conversation. I couldn't understand one word! At first, I thought they were speaking Gaelic, the ancient language of the Western Isles, but occasionally, I could make out some sort of English. I had passed on France because of my limited French language skills. Now I was in a country where I couldn't grasp what was supposed to be English spoken with a thick Scottish burr.

After a 5-mile taxi ride from Elgin, I finally arrived at the RAF Lossiemouth Officers Mess. It was magnificent. Instead of the tattered elegance of a typical old RAF mess, the facility resembled a new business-class hotel. The rooms were spacious and modern, the bar was bright and cheery, the dining room truly elegant, and the common areas well-appointed. Once I met some of the chaps, I asked tactfully, "What gives with this jolly-good Mess?" The RAF had within the past year taken over the station from the Royal Navy where it was known as RNAS, Royal Naval Air Service, Fulmar. A fulmar is a kind of shore bird, not what I would have named an air base after. Evidently, the RN built the mess to compensate for the miserable living conditions for naval aviators on board ships, but then was forced by the government in Whitehall to surrender the base to the RAF. Their loss, our gain.

One unexpected benefit of living in the Mess was my own personal batman. In the RAF, a batman isn't a caped crusader but rather an elderly man, usually a retired enlisted sergeant or naval chief petty officer. He was a combination of a manservant and a valet. He woke me every morning with a tray with hot tea and cookies. He took charge of my (limited) wardrobe making sure my clothes were clean and pressed and my shoes shined. If I was scheduled for a social event, I left a note on my mirror. When I returned from work, I found my evening's attire selected and laid out on the bed. That's the standard of living I would have liked to become accustomed to. However painless life in the Mess appeared, I was super glad when wife Pat and daughter Carolyn arrived after a month's delay and I could move out to be with them.

I arrived on a Sunday night and the squadron guys in the Mess told me there was to be an all-pilots meeting at 0800 Monday morning at the wing briefing room. At the proscribed time three squadrons' worth of pilots, about 40 blokes, and the Wing Adjutant, a Women's RAF officer, a bonnie Scots lassie named Wendy McGeorge, were present and waiting for we knew not what.

At exactly 0800, the boss entered the room. He was Wing Commander Johnny Walker. His call sign was "Whiskey." What else could it be? The adjutant called, "Attention, Gentlemen" and we all jumped to attention. The WC strode purposefully to the front of the room. He removed his billed hat and carefully placed it on the podium. He then looked out the window to the airfield where it was pouring with rain. He continued to frown at the weather for maybe 10-20 seconds then looked back at the adjutant and nodded. She spoke again, "Seats, Gentlemen," We sat down.

I didn't like the scene's vibes. Someone had screwed up big time and the WC was about to read all of us the riot act. I was relieved to know I had been on station less than 24 hours and whatever shit-storm was about to break couldn't possibly involve me. Whew!

"Whisky" Walker spoke, and I'm paraphrasing, "Gentlemen. The subject of today's meeting is checklists."

OK, I got it. This was the oft-repeated lecture on the use of checklists while operating aircraft. I heard the same ole refrain numerous times and I knew what was coming. Or maybe not.

The WC went on, "As you all know, my office windows look out on the tarmac where I can see pilots pre-flighting their aircraft. It has come to my attention recently that some of you are using a checklist for a pre-flight inspection and walk-around. Some are not."

So far, so familiar. Then would come the lowering of the boom on the miscreants.

"I presumed my instructions on the use of checklists were well-known, but evidently not. I would like to make my policy crystal-clear. If any pilot in this wing needs to use a checklist to perform his duties, he will be retrained so as to eliminate the need for such a crutch. Our men should know their jobs without reference to the written word. Have I made myself understood?"

What! Did I just hear what I thought I heard? There went 50 years of aviation safety teaching tossed out into the local downpour.

After a few more routine announcements, the all-pilots meeting concluded. Walker nodded to the young lady again. She called us to attention once more. He stalked out of the room followed meekly by the Adjutant. Welcome to the Royal Air Force, kid. I later learned Johnny Walker to be an affable chap, friendly, with a great sense of humor, a contagious laugh, and good report with his wing. Except about checklists. I lost a bottle of Glen Morangie Scotch whiskey to "Whiskey" in an ill-advised wager on the base pistol range. A great guy, but who knew Brits could shoot.

My new unit was the 226 Operational Conversation Unit, OCU. An OCU teaches rated pilots to fly an aircraft new to them. In the USAF, such squadrons are called Replacement Training Units, RTUs. As the Jaguar was just being introduced to service, the first two OCU classes taught the initial cadre. The third class, mine, would train pilots for line squadrons, except for me. As I did at the USAF FWS, I would go through the class and then stay on the staff of the OCU as a Qualified Weapons Instructor, QWI, the RAF nomenclature for a Fighter Weapons IP. Once a year, we would conduct a class for QWIs and I would instruct in that school as well, again like my job at Nellis.

In my time with the RAF, I never got to meet any of my boyhood Battle of Britain heroes. The closest I got was at a social event at a RAF base down south in England attended by Sir Douglas Bader. Sir Douglas was seated at the bar in the Mess surrounded by RAF officers. His crutches were nearby. Bader lost most of both legs when he tried a low-altitude aileron roll in the training command. He flew in the Battle of Britain with prosthetic limbs. The 20-30 RAF pilots in attendance were self-sorted by rank. Air Commodores and Group Captains were closest to Sir Douglas. Further out were Wing Commanders and Squadron Commanders. At the fringe of the scrum were Flight Lieutenants and one lone USAF Captain. That would be me. I never spoke to Sir Douglas Bader, but I saw him.

However, a GIB/WSO I Flew with at Ubon in SEA did better than I. Ken Schanke was a super GIB and an excellent light plane pilot, earning all the civilian ratings. He met some of the legends. His account follows.

Across the Channel in the Company of Legends
by
Kenneth H. Schanke

In March of 1979, the Red River Valley Fighter Pilots Association held its third European reunion at Ramstein AB, Germany. I was stationed there at the time in the 86th Tac Fighter Wing, attached to the 512th Tac Fighter Squadron. At the previous two reunions, the organizers had arranged for German Lt. Gen. Adolph Galland, and Col. Erich Hartman to be the guests of honor as well as the guest speakers at the formal dinner on Saturday night. In 1979, the guest of honor was Wing Commander Robert Stanford "Friar" Tuck.

As part of the agreement to attend, Wing Commander Tuck was transported by aero club aircraft, as he preferred not to have to put up with the hassle of commercial transportation (thinks like a fighter pilot). As a current member of the Ramstein AB aero club, I was asked to be the pilot for the flight. I was tied up in a local exercise for his Friday pick-up flight, but I made sure I would be available for the return flight on Sunday morning. Since I knew I would be flying early the next morning, I reduced my intake of intoxicating beverages at the Saturday night affair (it's a lie, but it looks good on paper). The guest of honor did his usual magnificent job of providing excellent war stories and anecdotes to entertain the assembled aviators. He did not however go light on the refreshments. Commander Tuck was a houseguest of Ken Cordier; Ken can provide many more stories about the very long night, conversations in Russian and running out of "pink" gin.

Ken delivered Friar Tuck to base operations early Sunday morning on schedule. You had to feel your way across the taxiway to base ops, as the day started with thick heavy fog. I had already checked with weather, and it didn't look good. The best chance of the fog lifting to at least takeoff minimums (200/1/2) was forecast for about 1300. We sat for a while at the cafeteria drinking coffee while getting updates on the weather about every hour. Commander Tuck was concerned as he had a business meeting scheduled the next morning in London, and "absolutely had to get home." (Get-home-itis has killed many a good pilot.)

Finally at about noon, the decision was made to go for it. Takeoff minimums were expected within the hour, en route weather was forecast for icing above 6,000 feet with moderate turbulence and strong headwinds below that altitude. The 30-40 knot headwinds were going to make it a long flight. But arrival weather at RAF Manston, U.K., was forecast to be good at 4,000-foot ceiling and four miles visibility.

According to my civilian logbook, on 11 March 1979, I logged 4.3 hours in a Piper Cherokee 180R, all of it instrument time between Ramstein AB and RAF Manston. It was quite possibly the worst flight of my life. Upon entering the clouds at about the forecasted 200 feet, I never saw a thing until on short final at Manston. I had requested from ATC a route that would take me north a bit over Belgium, knowing the air traffic control communications would be good. The clearance received directed me south over France. Not good. As forecast, below 6,000 feet it was bumpy and solid clouds. The outside air temp was just above freezing, so it wasn't possible to climb to get away from the chop. Fighting with maps, locating airways, and winging it to stay on course took two hands, but one was needed on the controls. Tuck, while a pilot, was no help as he promptly fell asleep next to me in the right seat. I had my wife and daughter in the backseat, and my wife was a great help in finding the right map, folding it as I explained, and handing it to me over my shoulder.

Once inside French airspace, as I expected, I could not get anyone to talk to me on any of many frequencies listed. It was lost com, in the weather, bouncing around, and fighting headwinds. It was not what I signed up for when I volunteered for this VIP flight. Once, an hour or so after crossing into France, a TWA flight replied when they heard me trying to talk to the French controllers. They relayed my position report, and provided an update on the weather. Half an hour later, I had a brief two-minute break of flying solid IMC (instrument meteorological conditions – solid clouds) when I broke out between layers. I was glad I was nearing Calais and would soon enter British airspace and at least have someone to talk to.

As I passed Calais and switched over to Easter Radar freq, Eastern called me before I could even call them. Loud and clear was considerably better than lost com, but I was still in solid clouds. The actual weather conditions at RAF Manston were way below the forecast. The 300-foot ceiling and one-mile visibility didn't bother me much, but the 35-knot quartering crosswinds were actually outside of the aircraft landing limits. As the winds were generally from the west, by mid-channel they had us on a direct vector to the field. I requested and received a GCA (Ground Controlled Approach [radar directed]) approach, and "talk down" (general call sign for English GCA) did its usual magnificent job directing me to where I could see the runway. The visibility was better than forecast, at about two miles, so I lined up on the upwind side of the runway and made a decent crosswind landing.

Commander Tuck was safely deposited, we said our goodbyes, and my family and I trudged off to clear customs and pay the required landing fees. While at base ops, I called the command post at Ramstein informing them of my intentions to remain the night and to tell my squadron I would be late for work on Monday. I was completely fatigued and mentally drained after the four plus hours of single pilot instrument time with no autopilot. There was no way I was going to take off into that again; besides I was well out of crew rest. We spent the night at a nearby hotel and enjoyed breakfast at a small inn in Ramsgate. The next morning the sun was shining brightly promising a much better flight home. In fact, with the same winds now being tailwinds and a VFR forecast, the return flight was logged at only 2.7 hours.

Old friends at Ramstein. Back row left to right: Friar Tuck, Bob "BC" Connelly, Ken Cordier, and Lt. Gen. Adolph Galland. Seated in front are Sir Douglas Bader and Heidi.

Like a glutton for punishment, I volunteered again to do the same thing the following year. Like the year before, I had another pilot make the pick-up, but I was on tap for the Sunday return. This year, our guest of honor was Sir Douglas Bader, and of course his "good chum" the Friar would be coming with him. This year at the European reunion, the Friday night flight suit party was really an outstanding affair. Held again at the base golf course club house, I was pleasantly surprised by the attendance of many of my friends from bases and places from the past. The Saturday night banquet was exceptional as well with three of the most famous historical aviators in our presence. As he had done since he was guest speaker a few years before, Lt. Gen. Adolph Galland was present at the party, as were both Sir Douglas and WC Tuck. I overheard Sir Douglas talking to Adolph about how small the aircraft had been for the flight over (the same Cherokee 180R). Sir Douglas joked to his old friend saying, "It was so small, I thought I should have taken off my legs to be more comfortable." Dolpho, the gentleman that he was, offered me the use of his Beech Bonanza for the return trip. It was a generous offer, but the aircraft was parked near Bonn, and the scheduled departure time precluded accepting his offer. I assured them all that I had reserved the Reims Rocket, a Cessna 172J (same size as a normal 172 but with a 200 HP engine that greatly improved its performance) that had much more leg room than the previous aircraft. I did one thing right that night and got a picture of the three VIPs and Heidi, Gen Galland's secretary and eventually his wife.

Sunday morning, the weather for the return flight was exactly the opposite of the previous year. 13 April 1980 was a beautifully clear day. I filed a VFR flight plan over Luxembourg, Belgium and again over Calais en route to RAF Manston. We leveled off at 1,500 AGL with Sir Douglas in front with me, and WC Tuck with my wife and daughter in the backseat. This was going to be a sightseeing flight. Passing over Vianden, Luxembourg, I circled the castle before heading for the Valley of the Seven Chateaus on the way to Bastogne. Over the monument at Bastogne, Sir Douglas stated that he had seen pictures of it before but had never seen it in person. We talked of the Battle of the Bulge, and he replied he was a prisoner by then and knew little of what actually happened. We continued to enjoy the time talking one-on-one as we too quickly approached the channel, which we could see some 50 miles in the distance despite our low altitude. Reluctantly I climbed to the required cruising altitude for the channel crossing and again was unable to raise France Control on the radio.

Soon we were over the channel and in the same airspace in which both Sir Douglas and Tuck had achieved many of their wartime kills. (Bader is credited with 20 kills and many more probable's, while Tuck is officially credited with 29) Thoughts ran rampant in my mind. How many pilots have ever flown in the same aircraft with either of the two Aces, let alone flown with both of them at the same time? I had already read Tuck's biography, and hoped to find Bader's while in England (I did). Most of the kills achieved by both multiple Aces occurred right here in this very airspace. Hundreds maybe even thousands of engagements between Spitfires and Hurricanes with these two heroes defending the coastline from numerous FW-190s and BF-109s, not to mention the deadly bombers set to destroy British targets. It was truly a moment to remember for a lifetime.

By now, Tuck had awakened from his nap, and as we neared the Cliffs of Dover he taped me on the shoulder and asked me to turn up the coast line, so he could show us his home in Sandwich, a few miles south of Manston. The published procedures required every channel crossing fly inland at least five nautical miles before turning, but I asked Easter Radar for the deviation. I made my request to the controller to fly up the coast direct to Manston, and with his most proper English accent he replied, "Are you aware of the proper crossing procedures?" I replied," I am, sir, and are you aware of the VIPs I have onboard?" Having included them on the flight plan, I was sure that he was. The reply was immediate, "Turn right and proceed as you like."

We circled Tuck's home, as well as his local golf course, then contacted RAF Manston for landing. Light winds from the west, so again the landing was from over water and the cliffs to the runway. Taxiing in I was directed to a small hangar not far from base ops. Aware of the arrival of the VIPs, Manston was ready with the photographers and they had moved a Spitfire out of the show hangar into the bright sun on the ramp.

Robert Stanford-Tuck and Sir Douglas Bader with a Spitfire, Manston, UK

While the local photographers took their pictures, I took mine as well. Until recently, I have never shared them with anyone except my family. We said our goodbyes and the best part of the adventure was over. Once the VIPs were gone, the base offered, and I accepted, the chance to climb into the Spitfire cockpit to "try 'er on for size." I fit, but barely. It was good that fighter pilots were smaller in those days than we are today.

As part of a planned vacation, we stayed in England for nearly a week, stopping a few days at RAF Mildenhall and at RAF Fairford, visiting friends and sightseeing around the countryside. Upon landing at RAF Fairford, we were met and guided to a hangar on the edge of the flight line. The doors were open, and inside on the left side of the hangar was a flyable B-25 that regularly put on airshows all over England. Once we shut down in front of the hangar doors, we were pushed back inside to spend our weekend parked under the left wing of the B-25. (The sad news about the B-25 was that only a few weeks later it crashed and was destroyed at an airshow when it attempted to complete a low altitude roll, only to impact the ground killing all on board.)

The weather was good to us the whole week. It was April in the U.K., and there was not even a cloud to be seen. The return flight home was also filed VFR. Like the flight over, the return flight was at minimum altitude enjoying the view of the countryside below. The weather gods more than made up for the previous year. My thanks to the River Rats for setting me up for the opportunity of a lifetime.

I was at Ramstein for just over three years, but managed to make four consecutive European River Rats reunions. Those were the really good old times. I still remain an active member of the Red River Valley Fighter Pilots Association and until recently served on the National Board of Directors as General Secretary. Old fighter pilots, and WSOs, never die; they just retire and spend time writing their memoirs as war stories.

The above account was extracted from Ken's excellent book, *Pigeons to Peshawar*, IBSN-13 #1460200360 by Kenneth H. Schanke.

I highly recommend it for a cornucopia of flying stories from very high altitude in the WB-57 to low down in light planes.

CHAPTER TWENTY-TWO
FLYING THE JAGUAR

Fierce Feline or Tame Pussycat?

In the mid-1970s, the Royal Air Force experienced serious decline. The force's point air defense interceptor, the English Electric Lightning, was obsolete as were its missiles. The most modern aircraft the RAF deployed, the F-4K Phantom, was wearing out and anyway wasn't really up to the challenge. The British government insisted on co-producing the F-4, nothing wrong with that, but also demanded the installation of a British engine. So, the Rolls-Royce Spey jet engine was installed, with difficulty, into the F-4 airframe. The Brits, unlike us Yanks, name their jet engines. The powerplants are named after rivers in the UK. The Spey, originally designed for use in civilian airliners, was several inches larger in diameter than the J-79, which was already a snug fit to insert inside the fuselage. Get your mind out of the gutter and erase the sexual imagery suggested by the above sentence. To make the Spey fit the Phantom, the fuselage was expanded, which screwed up the "coke bottle" profile. This aerodynamic "area rule" was a characteristic of mid-century jets, greatly reducing transonic drag. So, the UK Phantoms went from being Mach 2.4 aircraft to slugs which were barely supersonic. To make matters worse, the air intakes carefully designed for the J-79 were too small for the Spey, choking the engine. It was not uncommon for flames to shoot out of both ends when selecting afterburner, a.k.a. reheat, on take-off.

The replacement for the Phantom and the Lightning, the Tornado, while under development, was over budget, behind schedule, and under performing. At this time, the UK was undergoing serious social and financial upheavals with labor strikes rampant, inflation running over 20% per year, tax revenues down, and the Troubles in Northern Ireland festering. There was just not enough money in the defense budget to meet the UK's RAF commitments.

In parallel, and perhaps because of, the budget woes, the RAF's approach to ground attack ossified from a viable tactic to rigid dogma. The tacticians were obsessed with low-level ground attack by single aircraft. That's all they practiced. That's all they knew. The politicians reduced the RAF's theatre of operation to Western Europe. The grandees of the RAF reduced the tactical options to one approach; single aircraft very low and very fast, hitting targets on the first pass. This also relieved the RAF and the Treasury from having to fund the jamming aircraft and the air superiority forces needed for a medium-altitude strike force. Enter the Jaguar.

The RAF needed an aircraft to train pilots in the very demanding low-level tactics proscribed, but it couldn't afford the development single-handedly. The French Air Force needed a similar aircraft for advanced training but also as a trainer for landing on aircraft carriers. At the Whitehall level, a shotgun marriage between British Aircraft and Avions Bréguet was arranged to develop an advanced trainer, the Jaguar. So far, so good. When the Chancellor of the Exchequer, the Treasurer of the UK government, saw the new jet's projected unit price, five million pounds sterling each, he demanded the Jaguar fulfill an actual combat role as an interim replacement for the Phantom in the ground attack role until the problems with the Tornado got sorted out.

The Jaguar's initial design called for a dual-cockpit, light aircraft with efficient engines and lots of fuel on board, all the better to conduct long, low-level training missions. When the demand for combat capability came down from on high, two versions were re-designed, the T-2 and the GR-1. The T-2 was the trainer as originally conceived. To make a GR-1 single-seat ground attack aircraft, the T-2's forward cockpit was replaced by two Aden 20 mm cannons, an aerial refueling probe, and a laser range-finder feeding a weapons delivery computer. At least that was the plan.

When I transitioned into the Jaguar, it was just entering service with one short-handed squadron stationed in the UK and another in West Germany. However, the ever-present budget problems coupled with the need to get jets out to the field quickly produced a hollow force. In initial service, the guns were not installed as when they fired, they tended to crack their mounting bulkheads. The refueling probe was inoperative as it sprang leaks in the internal piping. The laser range-finder was nowhere to be seen. The bomb-aiming computer development had hit a snag. The promised electronic countermeasures system was still on the drawing boards. Worse yet, the limitations of converting a trainer to a combat aircraft were readily apparent to anyone who had actually flown in combat, like me.

The jaguar had no all-weather capability, no night ground attack capability, no precision-guided weapons, no self-defense electronic systems, and no air-to-air weapons for self defense. For a system assigned to ground attack missions in Western Europe where the weather is often rotten, where it gets dark once a day, where MiGs and Surface to Air Missiles, SAMs, were common, this sorry situation was seriously UNSAT.

It gets worse. The French/English boffins originally never expected the Jaguar to get shot at so they drew in some features which were, in retrospect, daft. The cockpit structure, the shell surrounding the pilot, was made of highly flammable magnesium. The pilot's anti-G suit was inflated with high pressure 100% oxygen instead of bleed air from the engines. The pilot's oxygen regulator was fed by a high-pressure line of pure oxygen. It resided on the pilot's chest. I made up my mind if I ever sensed smoke or any flame in the cockpit, I would instantly use the ejection seat to jettison the aircraft before a conflagration ingulfed my workstation.

To give the impression of some air-to-air capability, with no missiles, a lead-computing gunsight was incorporated to aim the inoperative guns. But with no radar or laser, the ranging function was provided by a scheme, stadiametric ranging, used on the WWII Spitfire. Yes, really.

Say you wanted to shoot down a MiG-21. First, in the midst a dogfight, you reached for a knob on the instrument panel and dialed in the intended victim's wingspan, in this case 23 feet. When the MiG's wings filled the outer circle of the gunsight projected on the Head-Up Display, HUD, you would be in range and the lead predictions would be accurate, sort of. But what if the MiG turned out to be a MiG-29 with a 37-foot wingspan, then your shooting would fall way short. Don't even think about engaging a MiG-23 with wings which could sweep back or extend outward. What a lash-up!

Another charming quirk of the Jaguar was a button under the glare shield, the Emergency Undercarriage Retraction control. All aircraft are prevented from retracting their landing gear/undercarriage while there is weight on the struts, all except English aircraft that is. During WWII, the propeller-driven fighters of the time, Spitfires and Hurricanes, had poor ground handling and weak brakes. It was thought desirable to be able to retract the gear in an emergency if the plane was headed out of control toward something important. This would drop the fighter onto its flat belly bringing things to screeching, if messy, halt. With low-wing, prop-driven fighters, this worked. However, the Jaguar was a long, slender, high-winged jet. If you yanked the gear out from under it while moving fast, it would, as the songs says, "Tumble and roll and dig a big hole." During ground training I asked the instructor to give me a situation in which I would retract the undercarriage on the ground. An awkward silence resulted.

Finally, the best/worst feature. When the French Navy was conducting sea trials with the Jaguar onboard an aircraft carrier, a serious problem arose when attempting a single-engine landing. The Jaguar's (small) Adour double-shaft, turbo-fan engines took a long time to spool up from low power settings. If a naval aviator was coming back aboard with one engine shut down and dropped below the glide path, things got dicey. It was very difficult to add enough power in time to prevent hitting the turned-down ramp or even worse, putting the jet into what the USN calls the "Spud Locker," the ship's ass end where once food supplies were stowed. The solution was to include Part Throttle Reheat, PTR, switches. These toggle switches, one for each engine, lit the reheats/afterburners if the engine rpm was above 83% for an instantaneous burst of much-needed thrust. The USAF Thunderbird's F-16s have this useful capability installed for air show precision flying. On the Jaguar the PTRs worked well except for one drawback. Instead of mounting the PTR switches on the respective throttles, as on the T-Birds' jets, the toggles were scabbed under the left canopy rail, sticking out horizontally. Leaving aside the cognitive problem of the engines, and throttles, being Left and Right and the PTR switches being Fore and Aft, they were located where your right elbow liked to move in the cockpit. It was easy to light the reheats by accident.

On my first solo, my IP, Chris McCairns, did a dual walk around with me, with no check lists, and a supervised start. Thing went well until I started to pull forward out of the chocks. I had brushed the PTR switches during my cockpit preflight. As soon as the engines reached 83%, both afterburners lit. That got everyone's attention on the ramp. My debriefing with Chris went something like this:

"It's extremely bad form, Mate, to select reheat when departing the tarmac."

The above accounts sound like the Jaguar was a total turkey, riddled with glitches and things which didn't work well. To be fair, the jet was rushed into service before all the bugs were squashed and before all the kit was fully developed. The UK just didn't have the time to wait, nor the funds, to do things quickly and correctly. In the USA, the F-104 Starfighter experienced the same sort of problems as it too was rushed into production before being ready. Like the Jaguar, the Zipper was initially fielded without its M61 Gatling gun. A lot of the trouble in the UK was due to having to coordinate every change with the French who had a somewhat different role in mind for their Jaguars.

Also in the mix was the workshare scheme between Avions Bréguet and British Aircraft. Each company was promised one-half the work and half the revenue. For example, the Jag's fuselage was built in two halves. One half was built in Warton, UK and the other built in Vélizy-Villacoublay, France. Then the two halves were swapped for final assembly at both locations. Leaving aside the waste in having two assembly lines doing the same task, a more serious problem revealed itself in flight testing. When pulling more than four Gs below 10,000 feet, the fuselage flexed at the joint where the two halves joined. This changed the length of the control cables and put in right rudder. The aircraft would then try to roll right with no pilot input. Very off-putting. The obvious solution would have been to build the jet's body in one piece with no seam. However, that plan would have screwed up the carefully balanced workshare. So instead, the flight control system was programed to put in a boot-full of left rudder under the noted in-flight conditions.

In the final analysis, the SEPECAT Jaguar was initially superb at what it was originally designed to do; low-level, high speed pilot training. You could, and I did, fly at 480 knots, 525 mph, at 250 feet altitude for an hour + 45 minutes. The aircraft handled well with no vices. It was comfortable and easy to fly with well-balanced controls and decent cockpit visibility. On the center console, between your legs, was a moving map display which made navigation easy helped by a good inertial navigation platform. The best feature was the HUD. This projected all the flight parameters you needed onto a glass on top of the glare shield. It looked like this vital data was suspended in space in front of the jet. The first time I flew it, in the simulator, I was blown away. Now even lumbering airliners have HUDs, one of aviation's best inventions but back then it was pushing the state-of-the-art.

To its credit, the Ministry of Defense Procurement Executive, MOD/PE, kept beavering away improving the Jaguar aircraft, trying to correct its obvious shortcomings. As the years rolled on, GPS navigation, a new HUD, a target tracking and laser illumination pod (for guiding laser-guided bombs), stouter engines, ECM gear, and Sidewinder heat-seeking missiles were added. The aerial refueling probe was fixed as were the guns and the laser range-finder. The Sidewinder launch rails were mounted on the wing's top surface, of all places. This was actually inspired engineering as it gave the 'Winder's" seeker an unobstructed view of the battle space so it could follow the also-added helmet-mounted sight. The strange configuration, as a bonus, didn't take up an air-to-ground, underwing weapons station.

The apex of Jaguar employment occurred during the first gulf war in 1991 which the US called, "Operation Desert Storm" and the UK referred to as "Project Granby" after a famous British cavalry leader. Twelve Jags deployed to the Gulf and flew over 600 combat sorties with good effect and lost not a single aircraft nor pilot. The aircraft were also more reliable and available during the conflict than the vaunted Tornado, their ultimate replacement. In later years, I ran across one of the Jaguars from the Gulf War. More on this in the pages to follow.

Once the aerial refueling glitches were solved, RAF Jaguars deployed across the Atlantic, and clear across the US, to participate in Operation Red Flag at Nellis AFB. There they gained a reputation for expert low flying. During one full-scale exercise, Chris McCairns called, and was credited with, an air-to-air kill on a USAF F-15 Eagle, which pleased him to no end.

But alas, the green eye-shade wearing bean counters at the Ministry of Defense Procurement Executive, MOD/PE, once again prevailed to save money and the aircraft were withdrawn from service, replaced by the Tornado, in 2007.

What success the Jaguar achieved was due in large part to the dedication and professionalism of its RAF pilots. At the time, one could join the RAF and be accepted for pilot training after graduation with what the UK called "A Levels" roughly comparable to a high school diploma with one year of college. If the timing worked out, it was possible for a student pilot to go supersonic before his twentieth birthday; a teen-aged Mach buster. I believe the RAF Lossiemouth Station Commander, a Group Captain, and I were the only pilots in the wing with college degrees. Late in my tour with the 226 OCU, we started to get college grads as junior officers to check out in the Jaguar. These guys were known as "Green Shields" due to the green emblem on their commission certificate indicating a degree. Sadly, the existing air crew resented these new chaps and made fun of them, perhaps out of jealousy or fear of replacement. Not a good scene.

But still, the RAF chaps were a dedicated lot. Inflation was running at over 20% a year. They hadn't had a pay raise in three years. You do the math. Most, without outside income, went into the red just to pay their everyday bills. At about the 10-12 year point in their careers, officers were summoned down to London to the Personnel Department of MOD, Air Force Section, called "Air Sect" pronounced "Air Sex." I volunteered to participate but to no avail. During the Air Sex meeting, each junior pilot was offered one of three paths forward: 1) Continue on your current path with the opportunity to retire with a small pension after 16 years of service. 2) Take the promotion track by attending staff schools and accepting staff assignments. Or, 3) Be designated as a "Specialist Aircrew" whereby one more promotion was possible but the pilot would continue to do nothing but fly airplanes, no command nor staff jobs, as long as he was fit. Most guys took the 16-year option, but by then they would have to take a more lucrative job to pay off depts incurred while on active duty. The Specialist Aircrew option was for folks who loved to fly and could endure a life with a working wife of genteel poverty.

The bureaucracy promoted the fiction the promotion path was based on meritocracy. I saw it otherwise. Then, the UK was a class-driven society, one's accent indicated one's social class and one's proper station in life. I could tell an officer's rank, or more accurately his maximum rank potential, by his spoken accent. All the Group Captains and flag officers, Air Commodores and up, sported a refined Oxbridge accent. The middle grades spoke in public school terms, and the Specialist Aircrews sounded like Eliza Doolittle before her speech therapy. It is possible the senior officers acquired their upper-crust speech patterns as they climbed the rank ladder, but I doubt it. It is very hard to change one's manner of speaking. I know of only one example, a high-school good friend, Sir Skip Bowman, worked to lose his East Tennessee tones. He ended up a USN four-star admiral, knighted by the Queen. Sir Skip earned his success through massive competency and intelligence, not his accent. Still, changing one's speech mode can be done with much effort.

A classic example was my next-door neighbor, car pool member, and friend, Flight Lt. Terry Bushnell. He was an ex-lightning pilot and a good one. His was a state school accent. His wife was definitely working class by hers. The UK has three tiers of secondary schools. At the top is private education. Unless your ancestors came across the Channel with William the Conqueror in 1066 BCE or your name ends with the Earl of something or the Laird of something else, you aren't getting in. Public schools are one step down. By "public" they mean "private." You can get in if you can pass the entrance exam and pay the tuition. At the bottom are State and church schools, run and funded by the UK government. Judging by Terry's accent. I had him pegged for Squadron Commander, max.

Of the few college graduates I taught, a class of four stand out. Two blokes were OK sticks. Another was one of those talented pilots for whom flying comes easily. He was good and he knew it. The fourth guy was the problem. He was extremely motivated. He knew all the tech details of the Jaguar. His route maps looked like works of art. He aced every written test. He was trying very hard. His problem was he was always a step or two behind the airplane. At 480 knots, 525 mph, and at 250 feet altitude, that flaw can be fatal. I flew his final check ride and he was on the bubble.

I hated to flunk him, he was working so hard and was such a great guy, but he just didn't fully hack the mission. Washing out would have destroyed him after all his motivation and hard work trying to cope. I told myself he would get more training at his squadron and would eventually come up to speed. Crossing my fingers, I signed him off.

Early on his operational squadron tour, Terry Bushnell hit the ground at high speed, leaving behind a grieving wife and a toddler who, like my daughter Carolyn, would never know her biological father. Terry was the first person to die in a Jaguar crash. He would not be the last.

In a year, two guys in the four-man "Green Shield" class were dead. They had both flown into the ground. One was the really proficient guy and one was the guy I barely passed. I often blame myself for him cashing in his chips. Had I flunked him, he'd probably be alive today working in finance in the City of London.

Despite the dangers of low-level flying, I found myself enjoying the challenge, sometimes more than others. One of the not-so-cool flights follows.

CHAPTER TWENTY-THREE
LOW-LEVEL LIFE

A Spot of Bother

Once I finished the basic conversion course on how to fly the Jaguar, I went through a short course, upgrading to be an instructor, teaching other junior birdmen to fly the jet. My final check ride was with the boss, Wing Commander Johnny "Whiskey" Walker. I found this to be extraordinary. In the USAF, by the time an officer becomes a wing commander, equivalent to a full colonel, whether on not they actually command a wing, his or her piloting skills have usually atrophied to such a degree that they are barely able to hack a notional combat mission profile. Service schools, staff tours, additional duties, liaison jobs, all take their toll of flying *nous* eroding that once-vital edge. Full Colonels rarely have the time nor the inclination to maintain top proficiency. They view their role in life, and in the service, as leading the organization, solving problems on the ground. They could be right about that.

There have been a few exceptions in modern times. Col Robin Olds of the 8th Tactical Fighter Wing of Ubon, Thailand led the "Wolfpack" from the front during the Vietnam War. He also shot down four MiGs. My friend, Col. Al Whitley, commander of the F-117 Nighthawk wing, flew solo, night combat missions to Bagdad, Iraq during Operation Desert Storm. Finally, General Tony McPeak, Chief of Staff of the whole USAF, flew single-seat combat missions in the F-15 Eagle in the Gulf. But such pilots are all too rare.

Perhaps our expectations were, and are, unreasonable. No one expects an Army battalion commander to lead a bayonet charge. No captain of a USN ship is asked to take the helm in a storm. But for some reason, fighter pilots like to see their leaders fly the same aircraft, take the same risks, and hack the same missions as line jocks. I had a lot of trouble conceiving of a USAF wing commander giving an IP upgrade check ride. It was even harder to picture a pilot-rated wing commander flying in the back seat of anything. "Whiskey" Walker did and in the process taught me a few tricks of low-level flying. Remarkable, that. Signed off by the boss as a Qualified Weapons Instructor, I began flying with students over Scotland.

Northeast Scotland, near Aberdeen, is a land of gently rolling fields, small villages, train tracks, a spiderweb of roads, meandering small streams, and golf courses. Lots of golf courses. To the west lie the Cairngorms, low hills marking the realm of the Scottish Highlands. Eastward is the North Sea. The land is ideal for low-level navigation/flying training. There are few hills to hit, no high-tension power lines, and plenty of landmarks to confirm, or deny, where you think you are. The only large town is Aberdeen, a sea port. There aren't many people to complain about RAF jets screaming very low overhead, except for golfers trying to line up their putts. In our route planning, we tried to avoid lying directly over St. Andrews, Troon, Glen Eagles, and any other sacred golf ground.

Once, flying as Number Two chasing a student on a check ride, I was at 250' AGL, 480 KIAS, 525 mph, over NE Scotland when we were bounced by RAF Phantoms. I broke hard right, pulling down and behind my flight lead's tail to clear his six o'clock and to give the F-4s more angle-off to convert. In full reheat with 4 Gs on the aircraft, I sailed through my leader's jet wash. My Jaguar flipped inverted, rolling 180 degrees to the right in less than a second.

I was looking back over my right shoulder with my left arm jammed hard against the throttles for more leverage to better see aft towards five o'clock when the Jag went inverted. The canopy rail rammed my left arm, already under the strain of 4 Gs, and snapped my elbow 30 degrees over center. That elbow was already weakened from a snow skiing accident. As when you hit your thumb with a hammer, you have a second to think about it before the pain starts, I knew this was going to hurt shortly before it did just that, big time. I unloaded the aircraft to -1G and rolled back right side up before the agony hit. Fighting the fog of pain, I managed somehow to get the nose above the horizon to prevent flying out of the sky and into the world.

The Jaguar, like the RAF's classic Spitfire, had a stick which only moved fore and aft. Aileron roll control was achieved by pivoting the top of the control stick left and right like a Spit. There was no autopilot. I clamped the stick tight between my thighs (insert the joke of your choice here) to keep the jet steady and laid my reverse-bent left arm on the left

166

consol. With my right hand, I gave the inside of my left elbow a karate chop, which snapped the joint back over center, bending it the correct way. However, all this trauma inflicted on my elbow paralyzed my arm. It was limp as a dishrag, useless.

The next item on my things-to-do list was to adjust the airspeed. The HUD showed we were accelerating through 600 knots, nearly 700 mph with the engines howling in full reheat. I was about to break every window in Aberdeen by going supersonic. With my right hand, I reached across and pulled the throttles out of reheat back to the dry power range.

One of the Jaguar's many human-factors deficiencies was the inability to adjust the throttle friction from the cockpit. If you drew a jet with slack throttle friction, the throttles would creep back to flight idle if you let go of them for any length of time. Once at idle, it took forever for the Adour fan engines to spool up if they didn't flame out in idle, which wasn't at all unusual. The Jaguar was definitely a two-fisted airplane. I had only one serviceable arm.

Jaguars came in two sizes, single-seat and with two seats. The good news was I was flying a two-place jet. The bad news was the rear cockpit was occupied by a RAF Flight Surgeon on his first fast jet orientation sortie. The poor bloke was sitting there enjoying the airplane ride, trying to keep his breakfast down when suddenly he found himself hanging from the straps watching the Scottish countryside blur by at 200 feet over the top of the canopy.

The Doc heard me scream when I snapped my elbow back in place. He came on the intercom ever so cautiously, "Ed, are you alright?" His voice was clearly fighting for control, that iconic British stiff upper lip coming through loud and clear. It would have been funny if I wasn't so busy.

I replied, "Doc, how would you like to learn how to fly a Jaguar, RIGHT NOW?"

I coached him where to find the RPM gages and asked for 89% with the throttles.

I went on, "See that little yellow handle on the left wall, that's the flaps. The longer one with the wheel on the end is the undercarriage. Put each of them down when I tell you to."

I figured we'd collectively fly back to RAF Lossiemouth and try a pass at the runway. If that didn't work out, we could always make a Martin-Baker ejection seat letdown and walk back to the Officers Mess, for a wee dram of Scotch whiskey, or six. However, I wasn't entirely in favor of banging out with a broken arm.

But, with the intrepid Doc working the levers, we managed to land without too much drama and taxied in to dispersal. By that time my left arm was returning some semblance of function.

Back in the squadron crew room, the Doc politely suggested that a visit to the infirmary with him for me and my bum arm might be in order. After the x-ray exam (bone chips, but no break) I asked him, "Doc, you aren't going to ground me, are you?"

He looked me in the eye and said, "Ed, I won't ground you if you promise never to involve me again in such a close-run thing."

Another sortie is etched into my memory for entirely different reasons. I was tasked to chase a student on a low-level navigation mission but the weather was rotten with low clouds, fog, rain, snow, scattered more or less over all of Scotland. The squadron commander, Squadron Leader John Henson, told the student and me:

"The weather looks too dicey for a student sortie. Ed why don't you fly the route solo?"

OK, ours not to reason why, ours but to do or die. Wasn't that a British tradition?

I launched off into the overcast and changed the mission profile on the fly, literally. The original flight plan called for a clockwise circuit of Northern Scotland with a practice bomb run on the West Coast. Knowing the low coastal plains around Aberdeen would be fogged in, I decided to weave my way through the central Highlands. I could have flown a few minutes, then pulled up into the clouds, emerged on top of the overcast, abandoned the mission as a lost cause, and called for an instrument approach back at Lossiemouth. That copout never entered my mind. Do or die, indeed.

Flying through the mountains in marginal weather sounds like one of the all-time bad ideas. It was barely doable only if you knew exactly where you were, which the moving map display between your knees told you. Once in a valley, which the Scots called "Glens," under deck of solid clouds, you could press on even with almost no forward visibility due to fog. This involved flying formation with the canyon wall on your left or right until the glen emptied out into flatter terrain. You had to know that particular glen didn't end in a rock wall. Not a technique for the faint of heart.

I managed to thread my way through the Cairngorms as the weather deteriorated. A few times I was on the verge of pulling up but decided to press on for another 10 seconds to see if the visibility improved. This made no sense from a personal survival standpoint. I wasn't trying to drop a nuke on the palace of whatever despot family was running North Korea. I was instead busting my ass to deliver a 25-pound practice bomb on a makeshift target. As the flying got harder, I grew more determined to hack the mission. Why? Just because, that's why. Why did Randy "Duke" Cunningham attempt lower and lower split-esses? I thought Duke was nuts then, but I fell for the same siren song of self-imposed danger myself. I was perched on the edge of the possibly fatal abyss of adrenalin addiction.

I exited the Highlands, then diverted east and crossed the Firth of Forth, a wide ocean bay, east of Edinburgh. Turning west, I transited the relatively flat, narrow waist of Scotland to the West Coast without too much trouble without overflying any large towns or golf courses in a screaming Jaguar at 200 feet above ground level.

The original mission called for updating the navigation kit on a prominent lighthouse perched on a point of one of the Inner Hebrides islands, then scorching south across the sea for a minute and 45 seconds to a bombing range in the water just off the coast. I found the lighthouse, inserted its true position into the nav computer and started following the cues on the HUD. If I could find the target, I would drop a single practice bomb.

The target was a 20-foot square raft floating a mile off a rocky promontory. The bare-bones range was noted on a circle shown on naval maps as a restricted area with entrance prohibited 24/7. No fishing boats ever allowed. With no anglers operating there, the fishing was therefore excellent near the raft. During the over-ocean transit, the weather cleared a bit. I could see about two miles ahead of the jet. When the raft came into view, I spotted two fishing boats near the raft, one on each side, about 100 feet apart. The locals, who were nobody's fools, knew no one would be dumb enough to fly a bombing mission in such appalling weather. They had seized the opportunity to bring in some illegal seafood bounty. The smart thing to do was to have aborted the run, returned to base, and reported the poachers. I didn't do that. After working my ass off, sweating bullets, just to get to the target, I was in no mood to back off. A 25-pound practice bomb, if it hit a small, wooden fishing smack, would crash through the deck and out the bottom of the boat, leaving an eight-inch hole clear through the hull and letting lots of water in.

I refined the aim point on the HUD, centering it on the raft, and pickled off the bomb. Passing over the raft, I cranked the jet around to see where the bomb hit. I noticed the two fishing boats with their prows up in the air, bones in their teeth (sailor's slang for white foam under the bow), with churning wakes behind them. They were exiting the bombing range at flank speed. The bomb missed the raft by about ten feet and one of the boats by about three times that. I didn't report the miscreant fisher folk to the proper authorities and they didn't report me to the RAF for bombing them.

The most likely return route was up the Great Glen along Loch Ness to Inverness, then east to Lossiemouth. Enroute, I passed over a Royal Navy submarine on the surface headed to the nuke sub base at Holy Loch, Scotland. The irony of basing subs armed with multiple death-dealing atomic weapons at a place called "Holy" evidently never occurred to the Brits. Feeling good about the just-completed mission, I circled the sub twice at low altitude and relatively slow airspeed so the guys on top of the conning tower driving the sub could see their Royal Air Force at work.

Another, more sophisticated bombing range was located on the north shore of the Moray Firth, the bay which leads to Inverness. Tain range was a controlled, scored range on mud flats bordering a shallow bay protected by a sand bar. A range officer in a tower could observe the bomb strikes by whiffs of white phosphorous smoke emitted by the bombs when they hit the mud. He would then call out the scores over the radio and later transmit them back to the squadron. Just outside the range boundary to the west was the Glen Morangie distillery, producer of excellent single-malt Scotch whiskeys. We called it the "Fighter Pilot's Whiskey." Why? The lead-in line to the range ran from out over the Firth across the sand bar then to the west, all the time the jet's nose was pointed right at the distillery. When you pulled off the target, the gunsight on your HUD went right over Glen Morangie. If anyone had experienced a runaway gun, there would be no more Glen Morangie single-malt golden nectar.

Actually, runaway guns were not very likely as the guns were not operative all the time I flew the Jaguar. We practiced strafing by pretending to shoot at a ground target, filming the run on the HUD camera. The camera recorded imagery when the trigger on the control stick was pulled. Later, back at the squadron, the QWI would view the black-and-white film and critique the student's technique, giving a notional score. This was called "dry strafe." Dry strafing was like kissing your cousin, the technique was there but what was the point. Unless, of course, you were from the South, when there might be a point to the romantic exercise after all. But we won't go there, shall we? Sandra, no offense intended, we can still be friends.

Besides flight training, the RAF boasted of having a state-of-the-art flight simulator. This was a mockup of a section of East Germany replicated, house-by-house, road-by-road, hill-by-hill in miniature on a table about the size of a tennis court. It looked like the world's largest model train set. A tiny TV camera "flew" over the board, transmitting its image and projecting it on to a screen front of a mock-up of a Jaguar cockpit. Sitting in the *faux* cockpit, viewing the moving image was supposed to give a realistic impression of flying. How you "flew" the simulated flight controls drove the TV camera. Now, simulators are all digital but back then it was an analog world. The simulator instructors, rated pilots all, had a boring job. They seldom got to fly a real Jaguar. To keep from going stir-crazy, they built tiny aircraft to the same scale as the simulator's display board, attaching the toys to transparent fishing lines on long fishing poles. They could then dangle the aircraft in front of the gantry-mounted TV camera as it progressed across the simulated world. You would be concentrating on flying the simulator, navigating across East Germany when in front of your jet, crossing from left to right would be a red Fokker Triplane, piloted by Manfred von Ricthoven, the Red Baron, pursued by WWI RAF flying ace Mick Manock in a Sopwith Camel. Fun and games in the RAF. I often wished the UK's taxpayers could see their Pounds Sterling at work.

I wondered why MOD/PE funded three expensive simulators, one for each Jaguar base. The money could have been better spent on things that were sorely needed by the fleet, such as guns, aerial refueling probes, ECM gear, and a variety of missing electronic gizmos. Maybe the simulator contracts were let when the jet was only committed to a training role. That is the charitable explanation.

When not dogfighting with the Red Baron, guys in the simulator often found other mischief to get into. One student, carried away by the realism of the giant train set, decided to fulfill every fighter pilot's dream, to fly under a bridge. Of course our hero forgot the TV camera he was looking through was suspended from a gantry. The overhead structure wiped out the model bridge. As if I needed any reminder of the international flavor of the Jaguar program, we hosted a group of flyers who were as international as they come. Up next.

CHAPTER TWENTY-FOUR
THE FRENCH INVADE SCOTLAND

Sacre Bleu!

As we and the French flew almost identical aircraft, the French Air Force, l'Armée de l'Aire, would come over to RAF Lossiemouth from time to time to exchange experiences, to fly over unfamiliar terrain, and to party a bit. The French Jaguars were kitted out more in accordance with the jet's original purpose, i.e., as an advanced trainer. Their jets had no inertial platforms, no weapons delivery computers, no laser range-finders (our RAF birds didn't either, but were supposed to), and no ECM gear (ditto), and no moving map display. Their two-seat models mounted an aerial refueling probe permanently on the aircraft's nose where ours had a pitot tube. That probe was an interesting feature. French pilots practiced aerial refueling, using the probe-and-drogue method, with an instructor in the rear cockpit. Only single-seat RAF jets could be aerial refueled. Students had to teach themselves to insert the probe into the basket trailed by the tanker with no coaching. Sort of like a teen-aged couple at the local drive-in movie theatre. Otherwise, the performance of the two flavors of Jaguar was very similar. Or so I thought.

I was tasked to lead a four-ship formation, two RAF and two French Jags, on a low-level trip around northern Scotland. I got the duty due to my experience in leading four-aircraft formations with the USAF. The RAF rarely flew in such "gaggles." The weather that day was marginal at best, but the French had to return to their base at Saint Dizier, France the next day. We couldn't wait for better visibility to launch the sortie.

According to the Met Office, there was a good chance we would have to air-abort the mission. The further south you flew, the worst the weather was, although the northern part of Scotland was not too bad. Accordingly, I briefed, in English, in French, and in "Franglais," the standard air-abort procedure used by the RAF. If the weather closed in on us, I would transmit on the radio:

"Pull up. Pull up. Go"

On "Go" I would light the reheats and pull the nose up to 30 degrees of pitch, climbing through the clouds. I would hold +30 degrees until the indicated airspeed decayed to 350 knots, 400 mph, from the 480 knots, 550 mph, planned for the route. Then I would hold 350 knots with pitch control until I emerged on top of the overcast. To ensure divergence between the formation members in the clouds, I would pull up on, and hold, the reference heading planned for that leg of the low-level track. My wingman, #Two, a Scotsman named Sandy MacDonald, would execute the same maneuver, only turning away from my heading by ten degrees. The Frenchman flying as #Three would do the same, only being on my other wing, he would turn ten degrees in the other direction. His wingman, #Four, would turn ten degrees away from his leader, 20 degrees off my original reference heading. This should have provided plenty of safe separation between aircraft as we individually fanned out and climbed for clear air on top. I made doubly sure everyone understood the process as it looked likely to be executed.

Take-off and join up were normal. The first few legs of the route were over the northern portion of Scotland, southwest of Wick. That area of the United Kingdom is almost deserted and nearly uninhabited. It is a land of rolling hills, some steep, with deep lakes, called "Lochs" by the Scots, and few trees, just open heath. You can fly for some minutes seeing nothing man-made. The only human features were isolated, ruined crofter's huts which were abandoned during the Clearances in the 18th century and a few snaggled-toothed stone fences. Up there, it hard to believe you are flying over densely populated Europe. I was sure the French enjoyed to trip as they were used to flying over France which is densely populated. There they had to always be mindful of the locals. Their enroute altitude over France was normally 500 feet, or the equivalent in meters, whereas our minimum altitude was 250 feet, lower if no one was watching.

Wheeling a four-ship through the valleys and hills kept me busy. Then we started down the Great Glen near Inverness. The Great Glen is a Claymore sword slash running diagonally southwest across the chest of the Highlands from Inverness to Fort William. Low hills comprise the wide valley. The floor is occupied by legendary Loch Ness. It is a good route, taking you from the north coast, the Moray Firth, to the west coast. It is straight as a string with no obstacles.

As we started thundering down the Great Glen, I enabled the HUD camera as I always did when flying over Loch Ness. If perchance I got a glimpse of the monster, I wanted to be ready to record the image for posterity. That would be a long shot. I had little faith in the existence of said monster. Most of the claimed sightings occurred late on Saturday nights when someone was walking home in the moonlight from the local pub. Still, one can't be too careful where monsters are involved, so my trigger finger was ready to start recording at the first sight of a sinuous neck topped by a reptilian head sticking out of the choppy surface of the loch.

We four proceeded down the Great Glen under leaden skies as the overcast sank lower ahead of us. We were at 100 feet over the water. I could tell from the way their aircraft were jittering that the French were not comfortable down that low even over flat, wet terrain. Up ahead, I could see a fuzzy fog bank hovering over the loch promising zero visibility. I had no choice.

"Pull up. Pull up. Go" I transmitted and began to execute the air-abort maneuver I had carefully briefed. Climbing through the thick clouds I focused on holding my reference heading. At one point, the cockpit grew momentarily darker for a second or two. It was not uncommon to encounter embedded pockets of rain or thicker clouds. These cells usually were accompanied by a bit of air turbulence but this time, no bumps. I thought nothing of it, but later the memory of the shadowed cockpit scared the shit out of me.

As we emerged out of the cloud tops and leveled off, I checked visually for the others. There was Sandy, #Two, about 300 yards off my wing, just where I expected him to be. On my other wing, nothing. No sign of the two Frenchmen. Holy Shit! Did they fly into trouble? I scanned the sky for them. There they were! Both French jets were on the other side of #Two from me. They had crossed over, through the formation, during the climb out. The darkness I experienced was the shadow of a French jet passing over my canopy at close range. Two French jets passed by two RAF jets while all were blind in the clouds.

Safely back on the ground, I led a detailed de-brief. Usually, these sort of joy rides were wrapped up with a light-hearted, "Was it good for you?" Or "Any comments on the flight?" or "'Let's de-brief at the Officers Mess bar." This time I needed to know what screw-up almost killed me. The truth finally came out.

With an inertial platform, RAF Jaguars flew on True North. All the cockpit indications were referenced to True North which made map reading easy as maps are oriented the same way. Without an inertial system, the French jets flew on Magnetic North, the direction a compass points to. The difference between True North and Magnetic North is labeled "Deviation" and varies widely across the globe. The deviation in Northern Scotland is ten degrees. When the French pulled up on their magnetic compass headings, the ten-degree difference put them on a convergent, not a divergent, course. Given Sandy's Scottish background, I had briefed a quad-national midair collision. After we sorted out the airborne mess, the rest of the French *liaison* visit went ahead much more safely. Bar stools almost never collide.

At RAF Lossiemouth, we trained an exchange pilot from the French Air Force. Strangely, the pilot, Captain Michel Ballu, came not from the French ground attack community but rather from the air defense forces in France. He was lucky to be alive in Scotland.

One evening, he was landing a Mirage jet at an airbase in Central France. On short final approach, the aircraft began to sink low on the glide path. As is normal, Michel added power with the single-engine thrust lever. Nothing happened, no increase in thrust. He jammed the throttle into full military power to save the landing. Again, no added power. Full afterburner was next, with the same result. The engine was stuck in a low power setting, unresponsive to inputs from the cockpit.

At the rate the aircraft was losing precious altitude and the rate at which the airspeed was decaying, Michel quickly realized he had no chance to make the field. Ejection was his only option. He pulled the primary ejection handle. Nothing happened. About this time Michel began to think this was turning out to be a very bad day indeed at work. Desperate, he yanked the secondary ejection handle which functioned, blasting him out of the doomed aircraft.

French ejection seats have two parachutes. First to deploy is a pilot chute about six feet in diameter. This small chute stabilizes the seat/pilot unit, then it deploys the much larger main chute and pulls the pilot away from the seat. Under the main canopy, the pilot floats gently to mother Earth. That is if there is enough air under the seat for all this to happen.

Continuing his string of rotten luck, Michel had punched out too low for the main parachute to deploy. Still sitting in the seat with only the pilot chute slowing him down, he crashed through the top of a wooden green house in the back garden of a local resident. The seat landed on a potting bench which collapsed onto a mound of fresh potting soil beneath it. All of this destruction served to cushion his impact with the ground. It was then that his luck rebounded.

The owner of the property was watching TV when he heard the crash. Running out back, he saw his smashed green house with Michel sitting in his ejection seat amid the wreckage. The civilian was the chief emergency room doctor of the local hospital. Michel, as you would expect, had broken several major bones, his back, and had suffered severe internal injuries. The ER doc's wife called for an ambulance while the physician began working successfully to save the French fighter pilot's life.

Michel Ballu was off flying status for a year and when he returned to flying at Lossiemouth, he was happy to be back. Even then, he moved carefully and it was obvious from hid body language he had been re-assembled from spare parts. The lack of flexibility didn't keep him from taking up golf in Scotland. A good guy and a good squadron mate.

CHAPTER TWENTY-FIVE
WAR GAMES

Wars are Won on the Playing Fields

The risks associated with being an exchange pilot were not trivial as the above example illustrates, particularly when accompanied by ineptitude. Before me, the pilot in my slot on the exchange program was assigned to fly the Blackburn Buccaneer, an butt-ugly ground-attack aircraft originally designed for the Royal Navy. My predecessor in the program, George Vipond, an ex-F-105 pilot, was killed in the crash of a Buccaneer. George survived 100 missions over North Vietnam in the F-105 Thunderchief, better known as the Thud (from Chief Thunder-Thud, a native American character in a kid's TV show). He busted his ass in a subsonic aircraft transferred from shipboard duty. After me, my replacement in the program turned in his wings and resigned his commission to become a minister. I'm not sure what that meant.

The accident rate for exchange pilots flying with the RAF was four times the rate for similar aviators in the USAF and higher than for native RAF pilots. Why, one might ask? No one really knows, but I have a theory. The USAF's set of flight operations orders, including safety instructions, numbers hundreds of pages. It is several inches thick. The equivalent RAF manual is 12-13 pages. Instead of relying on detailed orders and rigid procedures, the RAF expects its pilots to demonstrate what it calls "Airmanship." Airmanship is the attribute of learning your job well and exercising good judgement in aerial flight. The Queen expects the individual pilot to make correct, informed choices and not to rely on volumes of regulations which may or may not apply. The typical USAF pilot is used to following "The Book" and thus doesn't develop the personal judgement needed to make reasoned risk/reward tradeoffs nor to think through unfamiliar situations. Also, the flying weather is much worse in the UK than in the USA.

I read the RAF flight instruction manual in an hour or so. I hoisted aboard the lessons contained therein. No mention of check lists. I discovered there existed a classified appendix to the manual called, "Confidential Orders." This paper was off-limits to all but UK personnel, no USAF eyes were permitted to view it. Naturally, I was determined the read the Confidential Orders. What a revelation. The only instruction I took seriously was to not date enlisted women and to pay your Officers Mess dues. So, I didn't and I did.

At the 226 OCU, our standard operating procedures were very reasonable. If you assembled a small group of Jaguar instructor pilots, furnished them with pencil and paper, no make that bar napkins. If you told them to write down flying instructions for the wing, you would get what we had. Some examples were: 1) minimum altitude enroute 250 feet, IP to target run 100 feet. 2) No supersonic flight over land. 3) During air combat, no head-on, sight-on gun passes. The rest were equally logical. My first day in the RAF included the breath-taking briefing by the Wing Commander concerning check lists. Late in my tour another briefing I heard was just as jaw-dropping. It stemmed from the RAF's approach to flight safety coupled with a desire for realistic training.

First some background. In our American military, the defense of USAF airfields from hostile airborne attack is a mission assigned to the US Army by the Joint Chiefs of Staff. The Army is tasked to keep the Bad Guys from attacking our forward-operating air bases. The US Army deploys Patriot, Avenger, and Stinger Surface-to-Air Missiles, SAMs. To date, the US Army has shown no inclination to even attempt to fulfill this role. In the RAF, airfield defense is the mission of the Royal Air Force Regiment. The RAF Regiment exists solely to defend airfields. They are air defense troops who are part of the RAF and under its command. When I was there, the Regiment was armed with the Rapier short-range SAMs.

Seven miles from RAF Lossiemouth was RAF Kinloss, located on a short, stubby peninsula on the Moray Firth. Kinloss was a base for a large, multi-engined, submarine hunting aircraft, the Hawker Siddeley Nimrod. The Nimrod was an adaptation of the world's first commercial passenger Jet, the Comet.

To determine the readiness and the overall effectiveness of the RAF Regiment and its Rapiers, RAF senior management organized an exercise, a war game. Two Rapier units were stationed on the Kinloss airfield, one off each end of the runway. The Jaguar wing's mission was to see if we could simulate attacks on Kinloss without simulating being shot down by the Rapiers. The "Fight's On" command came at dawn and lasted until twilight. In the far north of Scotland in Summer, this was about an 18-hour window during which we were to devise and execute our airfield attack strategies.

During the pre-mission briefing the day before, an Air Commodore, a one-star general, gave the keynote address. He started by referencing the few rules of engagement mentioned above, all of which we agreed with. Then he dropped the notional bomb saying;

"Gentleman, you all know the safety rules concerning the attack of ground targets. However, we can expect any enemy, such as the Russians, to not know nor to follow these rules in the case of an actual war. The purpose of this exercise is to see how the Regiment performs under realistic pressure. Have made myself clear?"

I couldn't believe my ears, in his typically British understated way, the AC just thew the (highly reasonable) rule book out the proverbial window, giving us carte blanche to be wild, to take chances. To be fair, only OCU instructors, all of whom had logged many, many hours of ground attack practice, were to fly in the war game. No students allowed. We adjourned to plan the next day's brouhaha.

During the exercise, guys were trying to fly down fire roads, between the lines of pine trees at 50 feet. Other came in from over the sea at 600 knots, 700 mph, on the deck. Pincer attacks from opposing compass points were attempted. All and sundry were detected and engaged by the Rapiers before any simulated ordinance release could occur. The Regiment was "downing" Jaguars like swatting flies. A very sobering experience for us aviators.

The only even marginally successful attack was flown by a pilot and his wingman, who shall both remain nameless. This pair noticed that, true to form, all the planned Jaguar attacks were to be flown at low, very low, level. They also noted that a civil airway ran, at altitude, directly over Kinloss from Edinburgh to Wick on the northeast coast. The flight leader had logged many sorites of high-angle dive bombing. The dynamic duo flew south to Edinburgh, filed an IFR, instrument flight rules, flight plan enroute, and climbed to 18,000 feet. They followed the airway knowing the Regiment's radar would spot them and assume the two Jaguars, in close formation to present one radar return, were a British Airways flight from the Scottish capital to Wick and thus could be safely ignored. When overhead Kinloss, the Jag pair cancelled the IFR flight clearance with

ATC and dove at 60 degrees down at the targeted airbase. Yes, the attack was successful, but the two Jaguars were "killed" by the Rapiers while exiting the target area, a pyrrhic victory indeed.

During the exercise debrief, this semi- successful, Air Traffic Control-aided attack came up. The two pilots were chastised for ungentlemanly behavior. Some things just aren't cricket, old chap. The flight leader refrained from replying that it is hard to break rules which have already been suspended by an Air Commodore. Instead, he made the point that on the very first day of a notional war, with civilian aircraft about, such a surprise attack could be conceived. He sealed the deal by relating how the Israeli Air Force menaced Cairo, Egypt by flying close formation under incoming Egypt Air flights. There are no rules in a knife fight.

CHAPTER TWENTY-SIX
THERE'S NO BUSINESS
LIKE SHOW BUSINESS

Getting Tattoo'd at Greenham Common

The French Air Force wasn't the only participant in hazardous flight operations. During my last summer in the UK, the RAF organized a splendid air show at RAF Greenham Common to celebrated the Battle of Britain victory in WWII. The event was called the "Royal International Air Tattoo." Evidently, a "Tattoo" is, in English parlance, a type of military ceremony or performance, not the Tahitian-origin custom of inserting foreign substances under one's skin. The 226 OCU boasted of the RAF's designated Jaguar air show pilot, Flt. Lt. Whitney Griffith. He and I flew two jets down to England for the show. My bird was the back-up Jaguar in case the primary show plane became unserviceable. I had no assignment to fly in the air display which took place on a Saturday and Sunday.

The weather was perfect and the air show was a huge success. Over 50,000 air-minded people attended each day. Normally, to get that sized crowd in the UK requires two soccer teams in the Premier League playing to a nil-nil tie. All the European air demo teams were there: Les Diablos Rouges (Belgium), Le Patroulle de Française (France), the Canadian European team in F-104s doing a series of flat passes, and individual solo demo pilots from Norway, Sweden, and other air arms. Each day the British team, the RAF's Red Arrows, closed the show. The North American teams, the Thunderbirds, the Blue Angels, and the Snowbirds (Canada) didn't make the trip across the Atlantic. Also flying was every aircraft from the Battle of Britain including a Lancaster four-engined bomber and, of course, Spitfires and Hurricanes. The RAF's strategic force with its giant Vulcan bombers and Victor tankers made appearances as well as all the then-current operational aircraft. Whitney flew two excellent displays and didn't need "my" jet.

Aircrews supporting the show were gathered in a fenced compound across the airfield from the public with tables, umbrellas, and refreshments. We were discouraged from mingling with the English *bourgeoise*. We called our ad hoc encampment the "Pilot Pen." It was actually a great place to meet and greet pilots from all over Europe, to exchange "war stories" and lies (like there's a difference).

It was also a great way to critique other guys' air displays and an excellent place to see the airshow up close. One group of pilots stood out. The Frecce Tricolori from Italy were only too eager to criticize other team's efforts. The rest of us had to listen to. "That's not low enough. That's not fast enough. That's not close enough," all day delivered with a heavy Italian accent. I told Whitney these guys were verbally writing a check I wasn't so sure they could cash.

The Italians flew the Fiat G-91 a sort of three-quarters scale F-86 Sabrejet. Their team included ten aircraft, the most of any team then and now. They were scheduled for one of the last displays before the Red Arrows closed the show. After all the verbal abuse we endured, everyone in the pilot pen hung on the fence waiting to see the Italians fly. They did put on a good show using their large formation to beautiful effect.

As an aside, a large formation of aircraft is known in Italian air force slang as a "Bilbo" after the Italian general who promoted such gatherings with biplanes in the early years of aviation. The Frecce Tricolori or Tri-color Force named after the Italian flag, maneuvered their Bilbo with considerable skill, each G-91 trailing red, white, or green smoke.

At that time, most of the aerial demo teams performed a maneuver in which the formation entered the airshow boundary flying down the runway then pulled up into a vertical climb. Sometimes the solo pilot would follow the formation up as well. Then the individual members would split off into four different directions 90 degrees from each other. They would then complete loops and head back toward the show center. If the timing was right four aircraft would cross show center at the same time coming from four different directions. It doesn't take much imagination to see how things could go horribly wrong with this show-ending maneuver. The US teams used to incorporate this display in every show, but as the air displays have been steadily made safer, it has been abandoned for the most part.

The Italians did this crossover routine, only with ten aircraft, not four. It seemed the air was filled with G-91s coming from every direction, each trailing smoke. All of us watching were amazed. We looked at each other as if to say, "How did they do that?" No one enjoyed seeing a truly skillful air display with a degree of danger more than I. Today's shows by the Thunderbirds and Blue Angels are pretty, well done, and impress the civilians in the crowd. But in some ways, the approved routines have been dumbed down, even emasculated. But not the Italians. I remember being not impressed as much as being appalled at the risks they were taking. A ten-ship crossover was just too much. When they finished their display and returned to the pilot pen, most of us had left. We wanted no part of that debriefing. On the show's second day, trying to top even themselves, the Italians performed their crossover not over show center on the other side of the runway, but over the pilot pen. That scared me and I'm fearless.

I told Whitney after the show, "These guys are a serious accident looking for somewhere to happen." Sadly, this prediction came true. In 1988, at an airshow at the USAF base in Ramstein, Germany, three of the Frecce Tricolori pilots collided, close to the ground. One of the Aermacchi MB-339 light attack jets they were flying went into the very large, densely-packed crowd of spectators like a flaming scythe. Seventy people were killed including the three pilots. The fatal airshow was hosted by a UPT 68B classmate and friend, Lt General Larry Boese. He saw the whole disaster unfold from the reviewing stand. To this day, Larry is loath to discuss what he saw, pointing to the numerous accident reports as his last word on the horror he experienced. I respect that.

Monday morning, Whitney and I prepared to fly back home to Scotland. He asked if I was game for a farewell pass down the runway on departure. Sure, I replied. Taking off, I made sure to tuck in tight to his jet. In the RAF, they teach student pilots to perform formation take-offs by spending half the time watching the leader and the other half looking down the runway. This divided attention precludes very tight formations. In the USAF, if your wingtips aren't overlapped with your leader's, you're not trying. As we lifted off, I automatically added back stick to compensate for the increased drag caused by the undercarriage retracting and stayed in tight position. I hoped some of the airshow pilots were watching to see how we do it in the colonies.

Whitney turned left with me on his left wing, leaving the reheats lit. We proscribed a loose circle around the airfield, accelerating all the while, until we were once again lined up down the runway. I glanced at the HUD. The airspeed was passing through 580 knots. 680 mph, heading for 600 knots, 700 mph, flirting with Mach one. My leader lined up on the right side of the runway and descended to 100 feet. On his left wing, this put me lined up on the parking ramp, the tarmac. The smart thing to do would have been to reduce power a tad, slide over to Whitney's right wing, and fly down the right side of the runway. I didn't do that.

I buzzed the ramp at over 600 knots and at 100 feet. When we landed back at Lossiemouth, the Base Commander, Group Captain (Colonel) Robert Stuart-Paul, RSP for short. was waiting for us on the tarmac. RSP was a good guy and the chewing out we received, which the Brits call a "Bollicking," seemed rather perfunctory. I had heard worse, or better depending on which side of the discourse you are standing on. RSP had received an irate phone call from the fun Base Commander at Greenham Common. When I wired the ramp, I blew some guy off a ladder, scattered some equipment, and generally caused havoc with my jet blast. No one was hurt and nothing was destroyed but RSP felt obliged to honor the outrage of his counterpart. It was still fun.

CHAPTER TWENTY-SEVEN
NOT ALL PERIL IS AIRBORNE

How Drinking Saved My Life

Not all the games played at Lossiemouth involved simulated war and real fighter planes. I was a member of the base basketball team. We played in the Highland League against Inverness, Fort William, RAF Kinloss, Aberdeen, all the biggies. The highlight of our season was the Royal Air Force tournament. Teams from most of the major RAF bases gathered at an air base down south in England for their version of "March Madness." This required an all-day train journey for our team from the wilds of northern Scotland.

We traveled from Elgin to Aberdeen and changed trains there for the run south. At the Aberdeen station, our new train was backed into the platform with the last car nearest the quay and the engine out of sight in front. Naturally, we plopped down with all our gear and baggage in the first/last car and waited for departure. Then one of our more astute and thirstiest members pointed out that the dinning and bar car was located in the middle of the train. To obtain a mug of tepid, room temperature British beer or a fatty snack we would have to trek through three or four cars. That was clearly UNSAT. So, we upped sticks and schlepped all our stuff to the carriage just behind the bar car.

About a half-hour into the trip from Aberdeen to Edinburgh the train slowly coasted to a stop in the middle of nowhere. The engine had broken down and a replacement was being sent from Aberdeen. British Rail in ops normal mode. An hour later the train lurched forward violently for some 30-50 feet with a bang. I never felt such a shock on a train. Shortly thereafter, a mother and her teen-aged daughter came running down the aisle. The daughter had removed her blouse and her back and shoulders were blistered red with angry burns. The tea lady had been pushing her trolly through the cars. When the train jumped, her large pot of hot water spilled, burning the young girl. Her mom kept yelling, "My daughter has been burned and I don't know what to do for her!"

We realized we really should go back to the rear of the train and see what happened. When we got to what was left of the last car, a scene of devastation awaited us. Due to a lack of communication or a screw-up, the relief engine plowed at speed into the rear of our stationery train. The rear half of the last car was totally destroyed and the new engine was embedded in the front half covered with a mound of debris. A Scots man was there, he was in the forward latrine when the wreck occurred. The poor guy was hysterical. He kept screaming his wife and baby girl were trapped in the wreckage.

In the past, I have ragged on USAF and RAF survival training but I needed to change my tune. All that military conditioning kicked in and we got organized *toute suit*. There were 150-175 people on the train and nearly all of them were useless, not able to cope with a traumatic emergency situation. The civilians were frozen in place, immobile. The entire Search And Rescue, SAR, effort was comprised of the RAF Lossiemouth basketball team, an oil field worker/"roughneck" from Texas, and two Philippino nurses from a hospital in Aberdeen.

The nurses set up a triage/first aide station in the bar car. Off in the distance we could see a major highway paralleling the train tracks. One of our RAF guys was sent cross-country, scrambling over fences, and jogging across sheep pastures, to the road. He meant to flag down a car and get word of the train wreck to the nearest town. Of course, this was long before cell phones.

The rest of us turned to and began pulling apart the wreckage with our bare hands. We found the poor man's wife. She was crushed from the waist up, deceased, and crammed into what had been the overhead baggage rack. Her baby, about eight months old, was in some sort of plastic carrier which probably saved her life. The enfant suffered a nasty gash on her knee and various cuts and bruises. For some reason, maybe a concussion or perhaps shock, the baby was not screaming as you would expect. She was strangely quiet. We passed her along the human chain to one nurse who took her to the fist aid station. At last, we got the Scotsman calmed down enough to tell us there were no other passengers with them in the last car. So, we looked for the relief engine's driver. The cab was mostly intact but empty.

We walked back up the track, finding the engineer laying beside it. His body displayed that "pile of rags" look of a person who has met a violent end. He saw the disabled train ahead and he realized there was no way to stop in time. The engineer bailed out of the cab trying to jump to relative safety away from the coming collision. Tragically, his timing couldn't have been worse. He met a stone overpass bridge abutment head-on and died instantly.

After about an hour of amateur SAR, the authorities arrived and took command of the situation. Our basketball team finally arrived exhausted at the tournament site at 0200 for a 1130 game.

There is no doubt if we stayed where we were in the last car instead of moving closer to liquid refreshments, most, or all, of us, would have been smushed in the train wreck. Our original seats were completely shattered, gone. Drinking saved our lives.

But what about the tourney? We won the Royal Air Force cup. I still have my award passed out by WC "Whiskey" Walker. Not bad for white guys. After a fatal train wreck and an amateur SAR effort, what's a few basketball games. Our starting five featured four American exchange officers. Only the center, "Lofty," spoke the Queen's English. The RAF Sports Council, the wankers, noted this and passed a rule for the next year's tourney; only two non-Brits could be on the floor at the same time.

Chapter Twenty-Eight
LAST FLIGHT IN SCOTLAND

For Auld Lang Syne

Back at the home drome, my exchange tour with the Royal Air Force was winding down. On my last day in the squadron, my name wasn't on the flying schedule. It was a safety of flight issue. Like in skiing, you always blow out your knee on the day's last run down the mountain. Likewise you always bust your ass on your last flight. After the first wave of student sorties launched, squadron commander John Henson called me to the duty desk and said;

"The first sorties are off; no spares were needed. There's a cocked kite on the tarmac. Why don't you go fly it?"

He didn't have to tell me twice. Gee, my own private jet to play around with. I sprang into action and was soon airborne. I crossed the Highlands northeast to southwest following the hills. Then I made one last pass at very low altitude up Loch Ness. I had the HUD camera at the ready but no monsters were apparent. The weather was nice, scattered high clouds with clear air visibility as far as the eye could see. Exiting the Great Glen, I followed the railroad tracks at low level weaving through the western Highlands from Inverness to Kyle of Lochalsh, one of the prettiest town on the west coast. Skimming the ocean, I flew a low 270 degree turn around the town's peninsula and then checked out the Isle of Skye across the strait, looking for the ferry boat from the mainland to Skye. At the time, that was the only way to get to Skye on the surface. Now there's a Skye Road Bridge, what a great name, but many frugal Scots still take the ferry boat to avoid the high road tolls collected on the bridge.

Around the north cape of Scotland, the land is desolate and rocky with sheer cliffs overlooking a restless ocean. The sea there always seems to be boiling with high waves, eddies, and turbulence. The froth-churning water looks like it is trying to eat the northern edge of Great Britain. The locals think this where the Gulf Stream runs into Europe, or Scotland, but I have my doubts, particularly in the wintertime. It gets bloody cold then. I saved a copy of the Inverness Scotsman newspaper from one "hot" summer. The headline screams, "72 Degrees Again Today. No Relief in Sight!" You would think the Gulf Stream could do better.

I continued east along the north coast to John O'Groat's, considered by the UK citizenry to be the northern-most point on the British Isles. From the air, I could easily pick out the small white hotel built on the legendary site of a Scottish clan building. This ancient meeting place was an octagonal building with eight doors. Each side mounted its own entrance so the eight clan members, all brothers, could each enter without interference from any other kilt-wearer. Once inside they all could sit at an octagonal table with no head nor precedent. No clan chief would acknowledge the superior status of any other. Grown men built that.

Climbing slightly, I pointed the jet's nose north to Scapa Flow in the Orkney Islands, a short six-mile flight away from the mainland. Scapa Flow was one of the great naval bases of WWI and WWII. It is formed by a ring of five islands protecting the shallow interior sound from the brutal North Sea's fury. The German High Fleet of WWI was scuttled there after the war by the captive Germans themselves. You can still see some superstructures of sunken warships sticking out of the water at low tide. Before that, for five hundred years Vikings anchored their dragon's head-prowed, and proud, longboats in the Scapa Flow sound. There they prepared for raids on rich Christianity's lands to the south. No Viking wrecks are visible now. On that day, Scapa Flow was all but deserted, inhabited only by the ghosts of sailors long dead and one American who never felt so alive as when piloting a fighter jet.

I returned via the northern moorland between Wick and Inverness. Dropping down to low level again, 250 feet. I pulled the power back to pick up 420 knots, 480 mph, to save fuel. I didn't want this flight to end just yet. I flew along the wind-swept surface of fresh water lochs with nothing civilized visible on either side for miles. White capped waves passed under the jet's nose. In the clear air turbulence caused by the wild north wind being forced to follow the glen, my Jaguar shook left-to-right, a function of a long, narrow aircraft. The F-4 bounced up and down in the same conditions. The F-104, with its nine-foot wings, didn't move at all.

I passed a sheer cliff, maybe 1000 feet tall, falling down into the blue loch whose name I never learned. Standing on the prow of the rocky face looking down at my jet flying beneath him was a tall stag, a red deer, sporting an enormous set of antlers. These are the almost-tame, farm-raised deer which rich, fearless Japanese and German "hunters" pay enormous sums for to come to Scotland and shoot. Somehow killing handsome, unafraid ruminates (look it up) helps the visitors affirm their fragile manhood.

As the Jaguar rapidly passed beneath the stag, even from a distance I could see his rack of antlers pivoting as he followed my flight until the sight of the elk-sized deer was lost behind the aircraft. Someday soon after my flight, the stag was probably killed by a well-heeled German or Japanese businessman who walked up and shot him.

The day of the regal wild stag is ending, his kind replaced with corporate-bred livestock. Looking into the future of fighter aviation, I fear the era of what author Tom Wolfe called "The single-combat warrior" is also coming to a close. Fighter planes are becoming interconnected nodes in an information net controlled by people sitting behind computer screens far away from the action and the danger. To save money, but not lives, flying time is being cut back. More and more training and testing is done in simulators. Not model train sets but multi-zillion dollar computer-driven worlds. It probably isn't in the future cards that a squadron commander will tell one of his or her pilots, "There's a jet on the ramp. Go fly it."

Returning to RAF Lossiemouth, I passed by the Inverness airport and said goodbye to the comely female in the control tower. I assumed she was a bonnie Scotts lassie but I never met her. We were only radio pals and she had the sexiest voice in all of Air Traffic Control.

I will never forget that last flight in the Royal Air Force, in the Jaguar, and over bonnie Scotland.

Epilogue
POST-MISSION DE-BRIEF

The Rest of the Story

As my tour with the Royal Air Force wound down, A set of factors, professional, personal, and familial, not necessarily in that order, led me to the difficult conclusion it was time to change careers. One factor was the desire to live in one place, a good place, for more than two or three years and to see my daughters not have to change schools against their will.

Life in northern Scotland had not been pleasant. One very good thing happened though. My second daughter, Lisa, was born in Aberdeen, Scotland. This gave her a British passport and dual citizenship due to my posting with the RAF. If Scotland carries through with the idiotic idea of leaving the United Kingdom after 400+ years, she will have triple citizenship. Is that even a thing? I will say the UK National Health Service gave her mother, Pat, and baby Lisa excellent care, no complaints there. Also, it was free.

My two daughters ran true to form. Fighter pilots usually father daughters. I kept an informal count of the genders of the offspring in every squadron I was in. The percentage of female children ran from a low of 63% to a high of 90%. No one knows why. Maybe it's some reverse-macho karma at work. The only profession with similarly skewed demographics is anesthesiologists. My theory is these statistical improbabilities have something to do with constant exposure to pure, 100% oxygen. Of course, these statistics were compiled when all, repeat all, fighter pilots were male. With the welcome inclusion of female-type people into fighter squadrons, it will be interesting to see if this phenomenon still holds. Maybe the female pilots will have all boys.

Offspring's gender may not be the only thing changing in the world of tactical aviation. Fighter airplanes are evolving and so are their pilots. In the "Great War," WWI, aircraft were evil-handling sons of bitches to fly. They were unreliable, uncomfortable fire traps. Both sides lost nearly as many pilots in aircraft accidents as they did to enemy action. Their guns frequently froze up as did their pilots. Imagine being in an open cockpit at 21,000 feet over France during the winter. It was a time of wooden airplanes and iron men.

By WWII, which never was labeled "Great," Spitfires and Mustangs boasted heated, but not pressurized, enclosed cockpits. Most of the handling vices had been mitigated, except for landing. That was still hard with that great, heavy lump of an engine hung way out front driving a propeller that tried to kill you if you added power on short final. My friend Geoffrey Wellum (author of *First Light*) who flew in the Battle of Britain, wrote in his log book after his first solo, "A Spitfire has landed at Manston Aerodrome with me inside." At least the guns didn't freeze often.

In Korean War era, the first jet fighters took to the air. The F-86 Sabrejet was a delight to fly with honest, straightforward handling. The weapons systems now demanded more attention with lead-computing gunsights, radars, and then air-to-air heat-seeking missiles. Cockpits were pressurized for comfort.

In my war, Vietnam, radar-guided missiles joined the fray aimed by long range radars. Operating the aircraft with inertial navigation sets, radar warning receivers, and aerial refueling took more bandwidth and skill.

Now, the aircraft themselves are ridiculously easy to fly. I could teach any competent light plane pilot to fly an F-16. Modern computer-driven flight controls feel like they're wired into your central nervous system. Operating the aircraft's many electronic systems is what takes most of the effort. It's like flying the world's largest smart phone.

Today's fighter pilots prepare for their profession not by reading books by Eddie Rickenbacker (*Fighting the Flying Circus*) or Arthur Gould Lee (*Open Cockpit, No Parachute*) but by playing complex, realistic video games. Skills acquired transfer straight across to the cockpit.

The accident rate for modern fighters is way down due to vast improvements in reliability, pilot training, and aircraft handling. As I mentioned in the intro to this book, this is called "Progress" and it is a good thing. It is less likely now that a spouse or parent will answer a knock at the door in peacetime and open it to find, dressed in Class A blue uniforms, an Operations Officer, A Chaplain, and a Flight Surgeon there to bring the bad news that an offspring or spouse won't be coming home that evening. It's a different world now.

Leaving active duty, I took a job with the Hughes Aircraft Company, later merged with Raytheon, in international business development, selling tactical guided missiles worldwide. Once again, Howard Hughes had a bearing on my life.

Based at the Hughes plant in Tucson, I met the love of the rest of my life. Heidi worked as a designer in the electrical engineering section at Hughes. She was/is a model Ellie McPherson lookalike with an infectious smile and a zest for life. She also wore the shortest mini-skirts in Engineering, brains and beauty. We were later married in Berne, Switzerland.

After grad school at USC, I joined the USAF Reserve as an Intelligence Officer. Eventually, I retired as an Intelligence Squadron Commander. You might be forgiven for making the assumption there was some synergy between these two vocations. I did get to work with the CIA, FBI, and MI6 on a variety of covert intelligence projects. There will not be a written memoir on this period of my life.

Well maybe just one story. During what German Chancellor Otto von Bismarck would have called "Some damned foolishness in the Balkans," the cobbled-together country of Yugoslavia was coming un-glued. I was on active duty at Travis AFB, CA which is a transport base. We were trying to get C-130 turboprop aircraft into the Sarajevo airport to extract Americans in danger.

The 23rd Air Force command elements at Travis were worried, with good reason, about the threat missiles launched by the Serbs posed to our aircraft. I was tasked to brief the General in charge on that problem. I covered the number of missiles, their locations, the aircraft carrying them, the missiles' capabilities, and their probable tactical employment. I finished with a short section on how to defeat or evade the threat. After I finished, the General said:

"Colonel, that was the most complete, detailed briefing I have ever received concerning a missile threat to our aircraft. Can you tell me where this intel information was obtained?"

Me, swallowing hard, "Uh."

I tugged at my shirt collar with the tip of my index finger swallowed hard again and replied, "Yes sir. Uh. I sold them to the Yugoslavs." There went my USAF Commendation Medal.

As I have told a few bartenders, "Maybe just one more, story that is." One night in Switzerland, I was dining with a few Swiss pilots who were doing the testing of one of our missile systems. Switzerland hasn't fought in a war since 1847 despite having the largest army in Europe counting reserves. No Swiss pilot has ever flown in combat as a Swiss. The test pilots wanted to know all about what it was like to fly combat in Vietnam. I was extremely happy to regale them with recounts of various war stories, most of which are now in my books.

We were enjoying beef fondue. This is where you take thin strips of raw beef and using a long fork, dunk the strips in a fondue pot of beef broth simmering in the center of the table. Once it's done to your satisfaction, you devour the beef with various condiments, potatoes, and baguettes. I have always liked my beef rare, even to the point of steak tartare as described in my book *War for the Hell of It*. As the evening wore on, I continued my story-telling waving my arms to illustrate flying scenes. The beef strips were spending less and less time in the cooking broth. Eventually, I didn't bother cooking the morsels at all but rather ate them raw off the serving tray.

Remember the old TV commercial where everyone in a restaurant or airliner freezes in silence to overhear financial advice from a famous investment house? Suddenly I realized that all the diners within earshot had stopped eating and talking. They were watching me wave my hands in flight with beef blood dripping down my chin onto my white dress shirt. I wonder what they thought of American pilots after that performance.

The astute reader will have noticed I have occasionally referred to flying the F-104 Starfighter and the F-16 Viper, but there are no stories included in this book about those aircraft. The truth is I never accumulated enough time or sorties in either fighter plane to generate any print-worthy tales, good or bad. This is even considering the inevitable narrative enhancements. I can say that flying the Starfighter fulfilled a teenager's fantasies, at least the printable ones. I wasn't with the Tennessee Air National Guard in Knoxville, TN, but rather with the Luftwaffe at their base outside of Phoenix, AZ. It was fun just to taxi that sleek aircraft. Flying the F-104 made me feel like a real Jet Pilot.

I wrapped up my USAF career with the Arizona Air National Guard in Tucson where I got some time in the F-16. Flying the Viper at age 49 was what it must be like, how would I know, to date a porn star. There was more performance there than I could physically access.

Instead of shoehorning F-16 and F-104 stories into this book, I included them in my book, *The Pilot: Fighter Planes and Paris*. It's a novel for folks who never read novels. Besides hyper-accurate descriptions on what it is like to fly the F-104 and F-16, there are chapters on the F-4 Phantom, the F-86 Sabrejet, the Supermarine Spitfire, and the Sopwith Camel. The tales spring from both my personal experiences with the F-104, the F-4, and the F-16 as well as conversations with guys who flew all those old planes. Check it out.

Years later, after I retired from the aerospace industry aiming to become a world-famous author, I took my wife, Heidi, to visit the Pima County Air Museum south of Tucson. It is one of the world's best air museums, go if you can and plan to spend the entire day. You'll see airplanes you've only read about like the SR-71 Blackbird and the B-17 Flying Fortress.

I wanted to show Heidi the aircraft I flew including the Jaguar. There in a long line of fighters, was parked a single-seat Jag, painted pink. Not red, not rust-color, not ochre, nor russet, but light pink. During the first Gulf War, as mentioned earlier, the RAF sent a contingent of eight Jaguars to the conflict. The Brits, who are not bound by convention, nor by good taste it seems, did some ad hoc tests in-theater. They came to the surprising conclusion that the camouflage color most likely to blend in with the Iraqi desert sands was pink. Heidi's comment, "You flew a pink jet?"

For our 68B UPT class 50-year reunion, some of us still on the right side of the daisies met back in Big Spring, TX. It was good to see the guys and their wives but the town generated mental depression. After peace broke out in Vietnam, the USAF closed about half of its pilot training bases including Webb AFB. This cutback on pilot production resulted in, surprise, a shortage of USAF fighter pilots which exists to this day.

Shortage or not, there is one thing I learned as a fighter pilot. I was fortunate enough to fly with and/or know pilots from at least two dozen allied countries from Thailand, to Norway, to Iran, to New Zealand. The inescapable conclusion I reached is that all fighter pilots are alike. We have similar personalities, similar outlooks on life (we enjoy it) and death (we cheat it). We are interchangeable between aircraft, squadrons, and countries. The ultimate proof of this claim is the case of Russian pilot Viktor Belenko. He defected from the Russian Air Force and flew his MiG-25 to Japan. He asked for and was granted asylum status in the USA.

Viktor finished up his military career flying F-4 Phantoms with the Montana Air National Guard. By all accounts, he fit right in. But I digress, back to Big Spring.

Big Spring is dying. The loss of 1000 jobs at the airbase and hundreds of free-spending junior birdmen devastated the local economy. Main street is lined with boarded-up store fronts looking like missing teeth in a broken smile. All three Wagon Wheel drive-in restaurants/singles bars are gone. The ex-airbase is a federal prison and an oil well pipe storage area. The once busy ramp and traffic pattern are silent. When we were there, Big Spring wasn't rich like Midland and Odessa, but it was prosperous. Like many rural towns it is declining. That was sad to see.

I did have a connection to the prison. A classmate of mine at Chattanooga High School became an accomplished performer in the Austin, TX music scene. He got into the drug world and began dealing to support his weed habit. He was busted and spent four years in the Big Spring federal pen, in my old BOQ. His name, and I'm not making this up, is Billie Stoner.

Also in retirement, I joined a French club in our town of Paso Robles, CA. In non-pandemic times, we got together once a month for dinner at a local French restaurant, natch, to practice our French. One night I was chatting with a mature Vietnamese lady, a native of Saigon. That place, for the time being, is now known as Ho Chi Minh City. During her childhood and adolescence, Vietnam was a French colony. As one of the city's elites, she was raised to be bilingual.

She asked me if I had ever been to Vietnam. I replied I had, 100 times, but I didn't like it at all. Every time I flew there from Thailand, people tried to kill me. We then discussed my role in the war. She said;

"You might be the guy who bombed my cousin up near Hanoi."

I replied with a question, "Is your cousin still alive?"

Her answer, "Yes, I think he is."

"Then it wasn't me."

Thus ended the conversation and this book. Check six.

THE END

TINS

ACKNOWLEDGEMENTS

The following people were instrumental in the compilation of this book:

Ed Petersen

Mike Conners

Larry Boese

Ken Schanke

Bill Swertferger

Brian Schwartz

Carolyn Mitchell

Ben Lambeth

AUTHOR'S BIOGRAPHY

Bestselling author Ed Cobleigh has been a fighter pilot with the US Air Force, US Navy, Royal Air Force, Imperial Iranian Air Force, and the French Air Force. He also served as an Air Intelligence Officer working with the CIA, FBI, and MI6 on a variety of covert projects. His memoir, *War for the Hell of It,* is an Amazon #1 bestseller and his *The Pilot: Fighter Planes and Paris* gets laudatory reviews as a literary aviation novel. His narrative biography, *The First Fighter Pilot: The Life and Times of the Playboy Who Invented Air Combat*, was named best new WWI book by Amazon. His novel *Fly with the Falcon,* is a story of sexual harassment and peregrine falcons. *And* I *Lived to Tell the Tales: The Life of a Fighter Pilot* completes his memoir series.

Ed knows fighter planes, fighter pilots, and air combat well. His first fighter plane was the F-104 Starfighter and the last was the F-16 Viper. He flew 375 combat missions logging the same number of landings as take-offs. He has been an instructor at the USAF Fighter Weapons School, the USN's TOPGUN school, and the Royal Air Force Qualified Weapons Instructor course.

It has not been all flying and air combat for Ed Cobleigh. He also knows Paris; its people, cuisine, wine, and its ambiance intimately, having been there more times than he can count. Ed has visited 50 countries in various capacities.

His background as an Intelligence Officer allows him to ferret out details and make connections others miss and to see things meant to remain hidden. These penetrating insights are prime features of his books. In the air, in the intelligence world, and in Paris--Cobleigh has been there, done that. His books have sold 27,000+ copies in 12 countries and four languages.

Ed has been on the faculty of the of the Central Coast Writers Conference and he teaches classes on raptor aerodynamics. When not in Paris, Ed and his wife Heidi live in California's central coast wine country.

For more information on Ed and his books, visit the website below:

www.edcobleigh.com

BOOK REVIEWS

Readers are invited, requested even, to post a review on this book's home page at www.Amazon.com. Reviews need not be lengthy, but they should be honest accounts of how the reader perceived the book, the highs and the lows, the good, the bad, and the ugly. Reviews will allow prospective buyers to make an informed decision.

Thanks in Advance;
Lt. Col. Ed Cobleigh U. S. Air Force (Retired)
Fighter Pilot.
Call sign, "Fast Eddie"

ALSO BY ED COBLEIGH
www.EdCobleigh.com

Fighter Planes and Paris
The Pilot
An aviation/adventure novel.

The Pilot loves fighter planes, a beautiful woman, and Paris, but can only have one of the three. His problem is a beautiful, mysterious French woman who may be a spy. Why does she keep haunting his memories? In making his difficult choice, the Pilot remembers classic combat missions from WWI to Desert Storm while re-living past love affairs, but who were they with? Fast-paced in the City of Light, *The Pilot: Fighter Planes and Paris* delivers a tale of passion, air combat, and history. You are in the cockpit, in the bedroom, in Paris, looking to answer the questions, "Who is the Pilot?" and "Who is his Parisian lover?"

A Fighter Pilot's View of Vietnam
War for the Hell of It

A deeply personal account of a fighter pilot's life and his journey
into airborne hell and back.

Ed, "Fast Eddie," Cobleigh served two tours of duty during the Vietnam
air war, logging 375 combat sorties in the F-4 Phantom fighter/bomber.
In *War for the Hell of It*, Cobleigh shares his perspectives in a deeply
personal account of a fighter pilot's life, one filled with moral ambiguity
and military absurdities offset by the undeniable thrill of flying a fighter
aircraft. This is an unprecedented look into the state of mind of a pilot
as he experiences everything from the carnage of a crash to the joy of
flying through a star-studded night sky, from the illogical political
agendas of Washington to his own dangerous addiction to risk. Cobleigh
gives a stirring and emotional description of one man's journey into
airborne hell and back, recounting the pleasures and the pain. the wins
and the losses. and ultimately, the return.

The First Fighter Pilot

The First Fighter Pilot
Roland Garros
Life and times of the Playboy Who Invented Air Combat

In the Spring of 1915, a Parisian playboy took to the lethal skies of World War I, becoming the world's first fighter pilot. Never before had a lone pilot hunted down other aviators. Roland Garros' aerial exploits unleashed unlimited air combat and changed warfare forever. Before leaving French café society for the Western Front, the young pilot set aviation records, won air races, and introduced manned flight to thrilled crowds in the USA, Europe, and Latin America. In combat, he was shot down, escaped, and made his way back to the waiting arms of an exotic dancer. His decision-stay in Paris or return to the front lines. Garros needed two more victories to become an ace. The little-known story of Roland Garros' exciting life and his fascinating times is a riveting tale well worth the telling. Learn how a pioneer pilot of the Gilded Age descended into the man-made hell of the Great War. This narrative non-fiction biography delivers that stirring account right on target.

Love. Loss. Liberty
Fly with the Falcon
Sexual Harassment and a Peregrine Falcon.

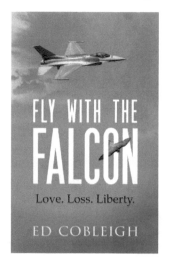

The boundless sky's peace and dangers are normally reserved for nature's aviators or for members of the elite fraternity/sorority of fighter pilots — or for readers of this new, fast-paced novel. Be elevated by tightly written, flowing prose to the exhilarating world of flight. Experience new insights into the world of the lucky few who view clouds from above. Follow the perilous life of a peregrine falcon along California's wild Central Coast and two fighter pilots, one female, one male, as they patrol the lethal skies of the Middle East. In this gripping narrative, each solo aviator searches for escape and meaning while airborne. For the three flyers, flight allows introspection into themselves and their terrestrial problems; sexual harassment, illicit sex, loneliness, lost lovers, and grounding. The coastal wine country offers a refuge and a path to discover what really matters in this world and how many barriers one is willing to hurdle to reach long-sought goals. Come fly with the falcon to discover the domain of the air, passionate romance, unspoiled Big Sur, dynamic falcon lore, and aerial adventure.

Made in United States
Troutdale, OR
11/07/2023

14369248R00120